Tourist Atlas
WESTERN

CW00672151

CONTENTS

In the mid 1600's the Dutch East India Company established a refreshment station at Africa's south-western tip to replenish their ships with fresh produce and meat. Over the past 350 years the erstwhile victualling station, situated strategically on the sea routes between East and West, has become a major African port, and a commercial, industrial and cultural centre. Cape Town is South Africa's legislative capital and the country's second largest city.

Cape Town is a cosmopolitan integration of old and new. Historical buildings rub shoulders with skyscrapers; cobbled streets contrast with motorways; the age-old Table Mountain looks down on the Foreshore area reclaimed from the sea in the last 60 years. Ascend Table Mountain by cableway, to catch the magnificent view from the summit, or visit the Victoria and Alfred Waterfront, situated around the historic harbour. From there, travel by launch the 11 kilometres to historic Robben Island, South Africa's symbol of liberation which was declared a UNESCO World Heritage Site in 1999.

THE DISA

Away from the city centre, the Kirstenbosch National Botanical Garden is a centre of indigenous plant life and research. The Cape Peninsula National Park incorporates Table Mountain and most of the Peninsula. Day drives to fishing villages, holiday resorts and quiet coves are great attractions of the Peninsula.

"LA DAUPHINE" BUILT IN 1804

Groot Constantia, on the Peninsula Wine Route, is South Africa's oldest wine farm. Cape Town's hinterland is a land of jagged fold mountains, separated by broad and fertile valleys. Stellenbosch, Paarl and Franschhoek are wine-producing areas of importance. Wellington, a short distance north of Paarl, was an original centre of the wagon making industry, and the terminus of one of the first railways from Cape Town.

North from Cape Town, the cold Benguela Current in the Atlantic Ocean spawns unhurried fishing harbours and villages along the west coast. There is still a little diamond prospecting and dredging. Pink flamingoes, gulls and gannets contrast with penguins, making bird-watching a most rewarding experience. Some stretches of the rocky coast are nature reserves, notably the West Coast National Park, Langebaan Lagoon being one of South Africa's finest wetlands, contrasting greatly with the nearby iron ore loading facility at Saldanha. Development in the south includes resorts and holiday marinas at which sailing is a main activity.

GANNETS ON BIRD ISLAND

This area and Namaqualand further north, are renowned for thousands of floral species. Within two months of the first rains the flowers burst into life, carpeting the land in a profusion of colour. The inland towns of Vredendal, Clanwilliam and Citrusdal are in the valley of the Olifants River, an irrigation scheme of note.

South-east from here are historic Tulbagh and Ceres, the gateway to the beautiful Ceres Karoo, a semi-desert landscape containing the Kagga Kamma, where a community demonstrates the harmony that exists between nature and the life of the Bushman. The Karoo is flat arid country. Matjiesfontein was established in the

1880's by James Logan as a health resort, and is now preserved as a monument. A night at its old world hotel is an unusual experience. The Karoo's dry climate makes it most suitable for sheep farming, and vast sheep farms cover the land. Beaufort West and Laingsburg are centres of the sheep and karakul industry. The Karoo National Park is near Beaufort West.

South from Ceres is the town of Worcester, in the midst of the Breede River Valley, and

THE KAROO BOTANICAL GARDENS

known for the nearby Karoo Gardens. The Valley, named after the river that snakes through the unspoilt landscape, is also an area of significant wine production, which is centred on Robertson. Route 62 offers a picturesque alternative to the N2 for travel from Cape Town to Port Elizabeth.

Still further south, is the Overberg region. On the N2, the main route to the Garden Route, Caledon is notable for its wild flower garden on the slopes of the Swartberg, and the historic town of Swellendam for the nearby Bontebok National Park. The Overberg region includes the town of Bredasdorp, and the most southerly point of Africa, Cape Agulhas.

The Garden Route extends along the southern coast between the sea and the Outeniqua and Tsitsikamma Mountains, stretching from Heidelberg eastwards to beyond the Storms River. The country varies from downs and wheatlands to the forests and lakes which constitute the Garden Route proper. This is the only part of South Africa with rainfall all year. Natural species such as yellowwood,

THE "HEERENGRACHT" IN CAPE TOWN

stinkwood and ironwood rise from an undergrowth of ferns and lianas.

European navigators knew the area around present-day Mossel Bay in the 15th century. The old milkwood tree in which ships' crews left and collected letters, the 'Post Office Tree', is in the Bartolomeu Dias Museum Complex in the town.

George was described by Anthony Trollope, the English novelist, as 'the prettiest little town in the world'. Not far away is Wilderness, one of South Africa's most beautiful seaside resorts; and the lake district. Knysna was established in the early

1800's by George Rex, a romantic and mysterious figure. The railway line from George to Knysna is a museum line, operated by historical stock, the so-called 'Outeniqua Choo- Tjoe'. The Transnet Heritage Foundation's Railway Museum is in George.

Plettenberg Bay, after a history that includes a period as a whaling station, is an upmarket resort town, whose population trebles in holiday seasons.

"HOLY TRINITY CHURCH" IN BELVIDERE

The Garden Route coast is rich in wildlife. Several nationally preserved areas between George and Knysna, attest to the importance attached to the ecology.

Knysna lagoon, 20 hectares of which is devoted to oyster farming, is administered as the Knysna National Lake Area. Featherbed Nature Reserve, on the western head, is accessible only by boat.

The Outeniqua Pass links George and the Klein Karoo town of Oudtshoorn, which in the late 19th century, was the world's 'ostrich feather capital'. Ostrich farming is a major industry in the area, and some farms are open to visitors. The Cango Caves,

SUNSET OVER HOUT BAY

north of Oudtshoorn, boast some of the world's finest stalactitic formations.

This book covers individually the eight tourist regions of the Province from page 30 onwards. These are: Cape Metropolitan Area; Winelands; Breede River Valley; West Coast; Overberg; Central Karoo; Klein Karoo and Garden Route. Each regional section contains detailed maps of an important area and street maps of selected towns in the region.

KIRSTENBOSCH BOTANICAL GARDENS

	BEAUFORT WEST	BREDASDORP	CAPE TOWN	CERES	CLANWILLIAM	GEORGE	KNYSNA	MOSSEL BAY	OUDTSHOORN	PAARL	ROBERTSON	STELLENBOSCH	SWELLENDAM	VAN RHYNSDORP	VREDENBURG	WORCESTER
BEAUFORT WEST	●	409	544	418	451	198	205	231	159	473	375	496	332	477	565	414
BREDASDORP	409	●	213	168	322	303	356	258	288	166	92	164	78	392	319	132
CAPE TOWN	544	213	●	129	222	495	544	455	466	72	180	53	249	286	132	131
CERES	418	168	129	●	155	392	445	358	356	61	87	90	161	227	170	36
CLANWILLIAM	451	322	222	155	●	488	534	466	442	190	233	216	297	72	143	191
GEORGE	198	303	495	392	488	●	67	49	54	429	316	442	247	539	561	371
KNYSNA	205	356	544	445	534	67	●	107	109	480	372	493	304	580	607	425
MOSSEL BAY	231	258	455	358	466	49	107	●	72	391	279	402	207	520	528	335
OUDTSHOORN	159	288	466	356	442	54	109	72	●	398	286	414	222	489	522	338
PAARL	473	166	72	61	190	429	480	391	398	●	113	30	185	260	153	60
ROBERTSON	375	92	180	87	233	316	372	279	286	113	●	127	75	303	254	57
STELLENBOSCH	496	164	53	90	216	442	493	402	414	30	127	●	196	286	162	82
SWELLENDAM	332	78	249	161	297	247	304	207	222	185	75	196	●	363	329	132
VAN RHYNSDORP	477	392	286	227	72	539	580	520	489	260	303	286	363	●	185	263
VREDENBURG	565	319	132	170	143	561	607	528	522	153	254	162	329	185	●	198
WORCESTER	414	132	131	36	191	371	425	335	338	60	57	82	132	263	198	●

Distances in Kilometres

* This distance table has been computer-generated

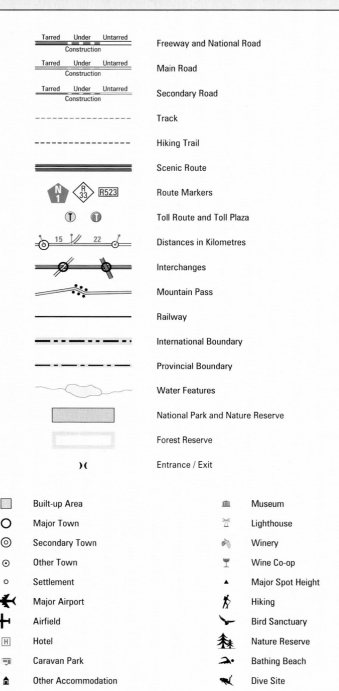

Tarred Under Untarred — Construction	Freeway and National Road
Tarred Under Untarred — Construction	Main Road
Tarred Under Untarred — Construction	Secondary Road
	Track
	Hiking Trail
	Scenic Route
N1, R33, R523	Route Markers
T T	Toll Route and Toll Plaza
15 22	Distances in Kilometres
	Interchanges
	Mountain Pass
	Railway
	International Boundary
	Provincial Boundary
	Water Features
	National Park and Nature Reserve
	Forest Reserve
)(	Entrance / Exit

▪	Built-up Area	🏛	Museum
O	Major Town		Lighthouse
◎	Secondary Town		Winery
⊙	Other Town	♀	Wine Co-op
○	Settlement	▲	Major Spot Height
✈	Major Airport		Hiking
⊢	Airfield		Bird Sanctuary
H	Hotel		Nature Reserve
	Caravan Park		Bathing Beach
	Other Accommodation		Dive Site
i	Tourist Information		Whale Watching
▲	Place of Interest		Shipwreck
★	Historical Site		Mineral Bath
	Provincial Heritage Site		Marsh

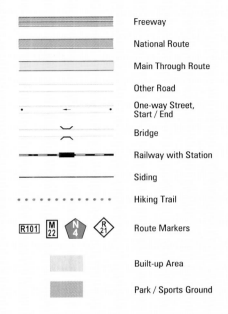

	Freeway
	National Route
	Main Through Route
	Other Road
	One-way Street, Start / End
	Bridge
	Railway with Station
	Siding
	Hiking Trail
R101 M22 N4 R21	Route Markers
	Built-up Area
	Park / Sports Ground

Airport / Airfield			Police Station
Hotel			Fire Station
Other Accomodation			Hospital / Clinic with Casualty
Caravan Park			Hospital / Clinic
Tourist Information			Community Service
Place of Interest			School
Provincial Heritage Site			Winery
Historical Monument / Site			Wine Co-op
Museum / Art Gallery / Exhibition Centre			Shipwreck
Theatre			Bathing Beach
Cinema / Drive-In			Whale Watching
Shopping Centre			Dive Site
Parking			Lighthouse
Traffic Light			Surfing
Entrance / Exit			Fishing
Post Office			Hiking

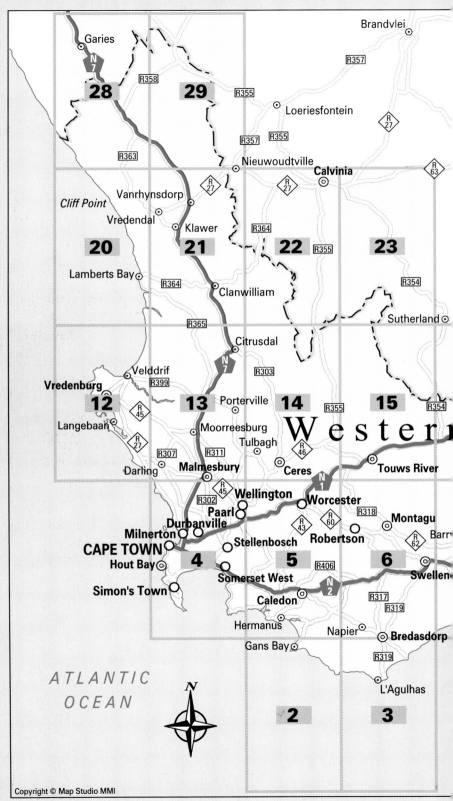

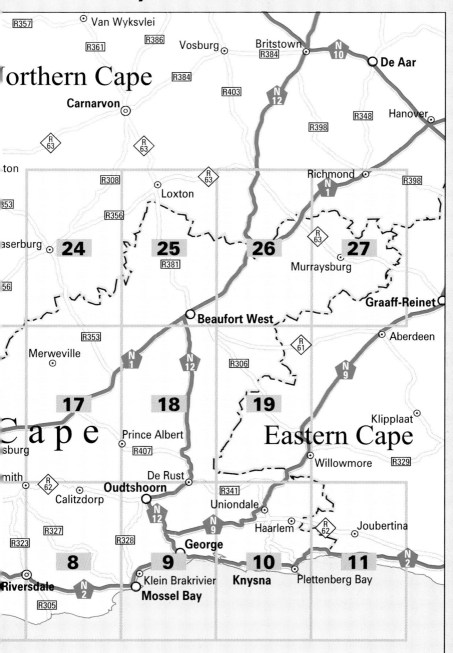

19° 00'

1

5

Stanford 20km   19° 30'

2

13

Walker Bay

R
43

A

Die Kelders

6

Baardskeerdersbos

3

5   2

Gans Bay

Uilenkraalmond

6

Kleinbaai

Danger Point

13

9

Walker Bay

Pearly Beach

Viljoer

Nature Reserve

14

R
43

3

Buffeljags

Jessie se Baai

Die

Quoin Po

SEE PAGES 90-93

ATLANTIC

OCEAN

35° 00'

B

+

+

Extensive wheat fields near Botrivier   See Page 5

C

35° 30'

D

+

+

19° 00'

1

2

19° 30'

tarred   under   untarred
construction

**Freeway &
National Road**

N
1

R
33

R523

Secondary Road

15

22

Distances in Kilo

Main Road

Route Markers

Mountain Passe

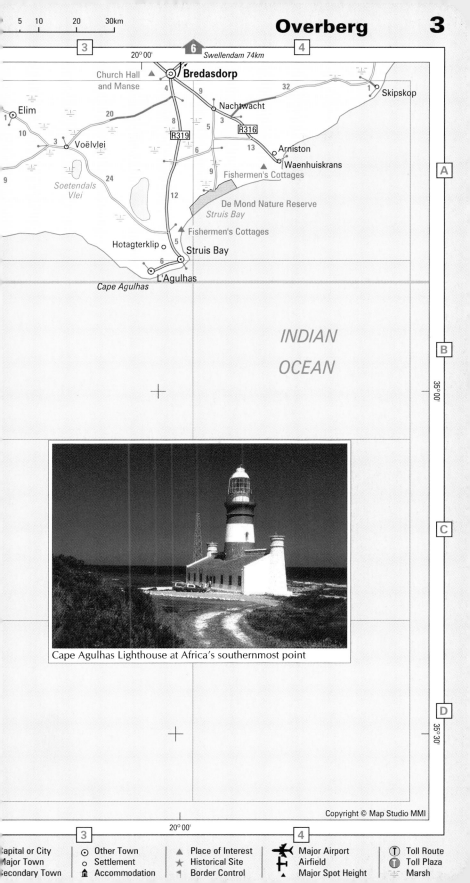

Scale: 5 10 20 30km

Church Hall and Manse

Bredasdorp

Elim

Nachtwacht

Skipskop

32

1

Voëlvlei

20

10

3

R319

8

5

R316

3

9

6

13

Arniston

Waenhuiskrans

Soetendals Vlei

24

9

Fishermen's Cottages

12

De Mond Nature Reserve
Struis Bay

Fishermen's Cottages

Hotagterklip

5

Struis Bay

6

L'Agulhas

Cape Agulhas

INDIAN OCEAN

35° 00'

Cape Agulhas Lighthouse at Africa's southernmost point

35° 30'

20° 00'

Capital or City	⊙ Other Town	▲ Place of Interest
Major Town	○ Settlement	★ Historical Site
Secondary Town	🏛 Accommodation	◄ Border Control

Major Airport
Airfield
Major Spot Height

Ⓣ Toll Route
Ⓣ Toll Plaza
Marsh

A   B   C   D

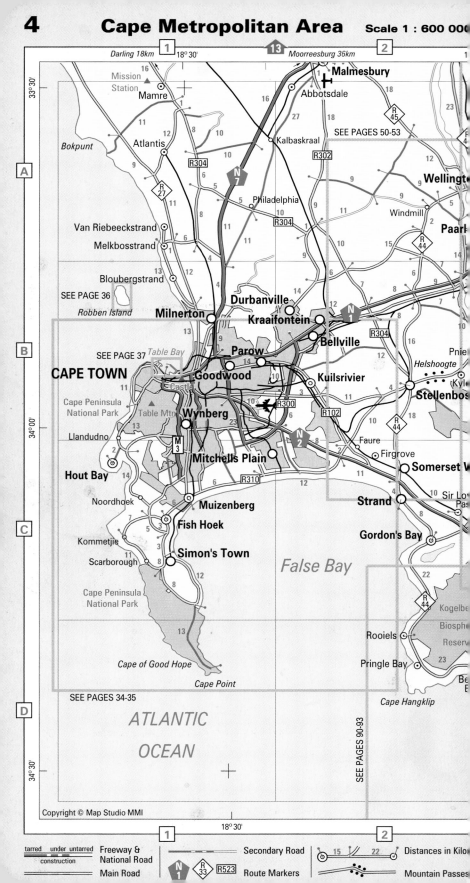

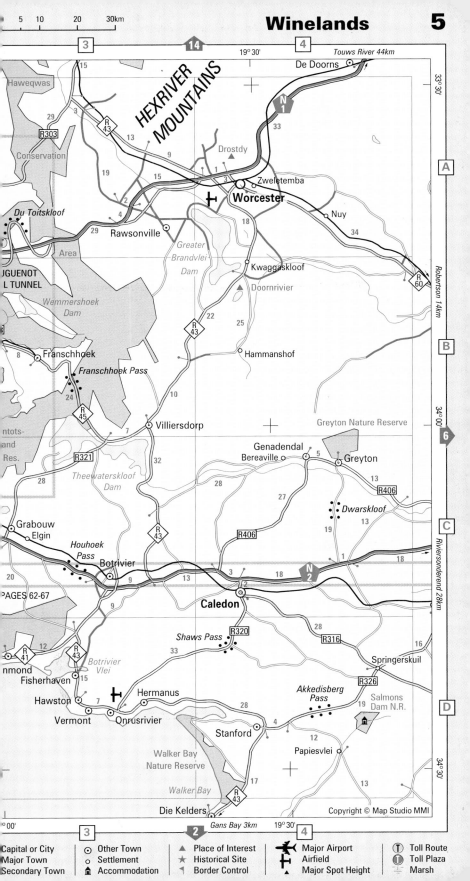

Scale

5 10 20 30km

Haweqwas

HEXRIVER MOUNTAINS

De Doorns

N1

15

29

R303

3

R43

13

9

33

Drostdy

Zweletemba

A

33° 30'

Conservation

19

15

3

Worcester

18

Nuy

34

2

4

Du Toitskloof

29

Rawsonville

Greater
Brandvlei
Dam

Kwaggaskloof

Doornrivier

Robertson 14km

R60

Area

JGUENOT
L TUNNEL

Wemmershoek
Dam

22

R43

25

Hammanshof

B

34° 00'

8

Franschhoek

Franschhoek Pass

24

10

Greyton Nature Reserve

R45

ntots-
and
Res.

7

Villiersdorp

Genadendal
Bereaville

5

Greyton

6

R321

32

13

R406

28

*Theewaterskloof
Dam*

28

27

Dwarskloof

13

Grabouw
Elgin

R43

R406

19

13

C

*Houhoek
Pass*

Botrivier

1

18

Riviersonderend 28km

20

PAGES 62-67

9

13

3

18

N2

9

Caledon

2

R320

28

R316

16

Shaws Pass

R326

33

Springerskuil

nmond

R41

R43

*Botrivier
Vlei*

*Akkedisberg
Pass*

19

Salmons
Dam N.R.

D

Fisherhaven

15

Hermanus

28

4

Hawston

7

12

Vermont

Onrusrivier

Stanford

Papiesvlei

Walker Bay
Nature Reserve

17

13

34° 30'

Walker Bay

R43

Die Kelders

Copyright © Map Studio MMI

Capital or City	⊙ Other Town	▲ Place of Interest
Major Town	○ Settlement	★ Historical Site
Secondary Town	▥ Accommodation	◀ Border Control

Major Airport
Airfield
Major Spot Height

Ⓣ Toll Route
Ⓣ Toll Plaza
Marsh

Scale 1 : 600 000

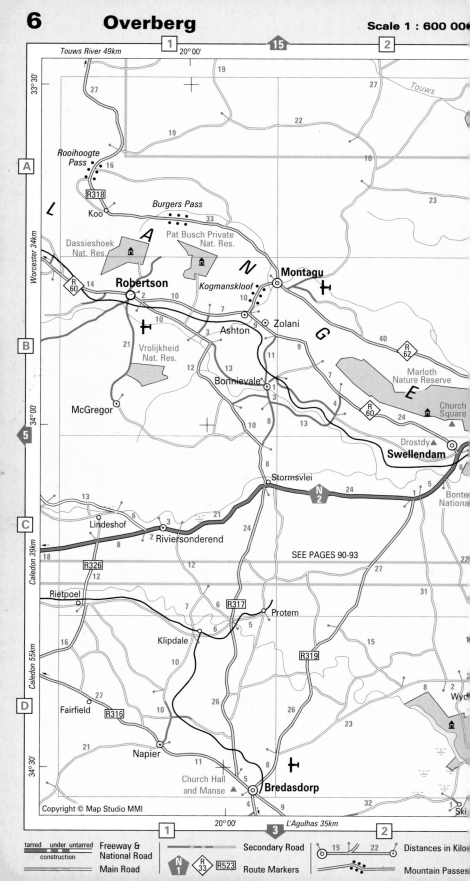

Touws River 49km

20° 00'

33° 30'

19

27

19

27

Touws

22

10

Rooihoogte
Pass

16

23

L

R318

Koo

Burgers Pass

33

A

Dassieshoek
Nat. Res.

Pat Busch Private
Nat. Res.

N

R60

14

Robertson

2

Montagu

Kogmanskloof

10

10

7

9

G

40

R62

Ashton

Zolani

9

E

21

Vrolijkheid
Nat. Res.

12

11

Marloth
Nature Reserve

13

Bonnievale

7

Church
Square

McGregor

1

3

R60

24

Drostdy

10

8

13

Swellendam

34° 00'

5

8

Stormsvlei

N2

24

1

5

Bonte
National

13

21

N2

6

Lindeshof

3

2

Riviersonderend

24

27

31

22

18

R326

12

SEE PAGES 90-93

12

Rietpoel

7

6

R317

Protem

16

6

5

15

Klipdale

10

R319

Fairfield

R316

27

10

26

26

23

Wyd

8

2

Napier

21

11

8

34° 30'

Church Hall
and Manse

5

Bredasdorp

4

9

32

Ski

Worcester 34km

Caledon 39km

Caledon 55km

Copyright © Map Studio MMI

20° 00'

3

L'Agulhas 35km

2

tarred   under   untarred
construction   **Freeway &
National Road**   **Main Road**

N1   R33   R523   **Route Markers**

Secondary Road

15   22   **Distances in Kilo**

Mountain Passes

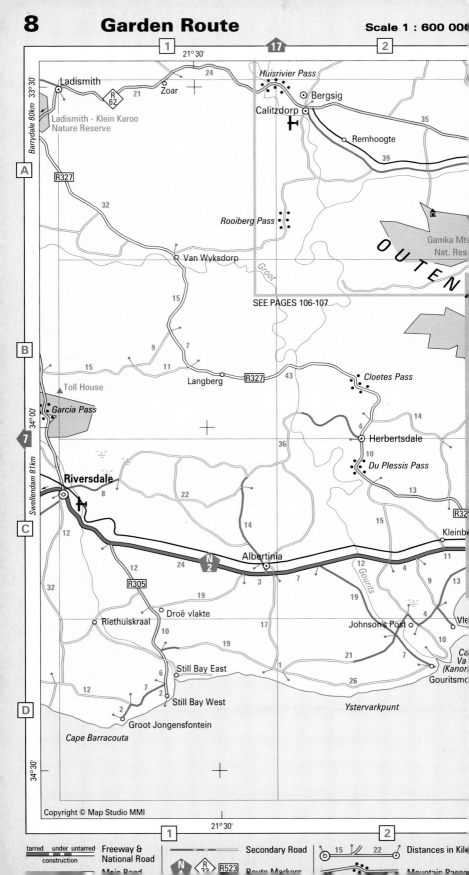

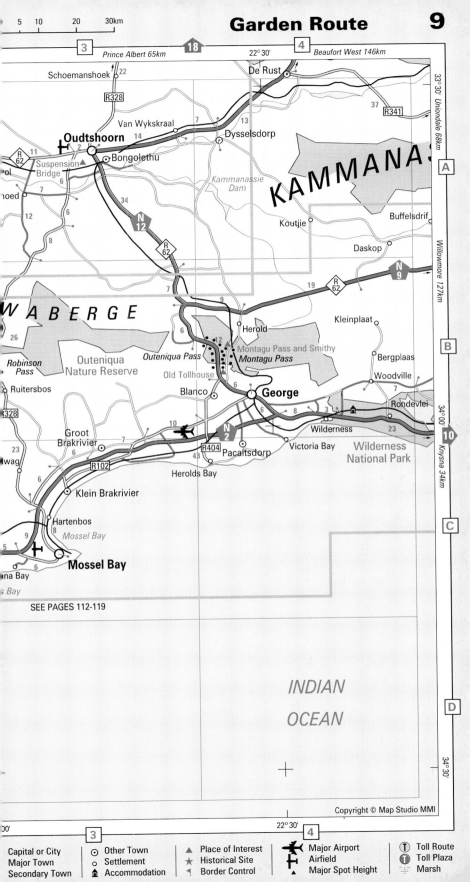

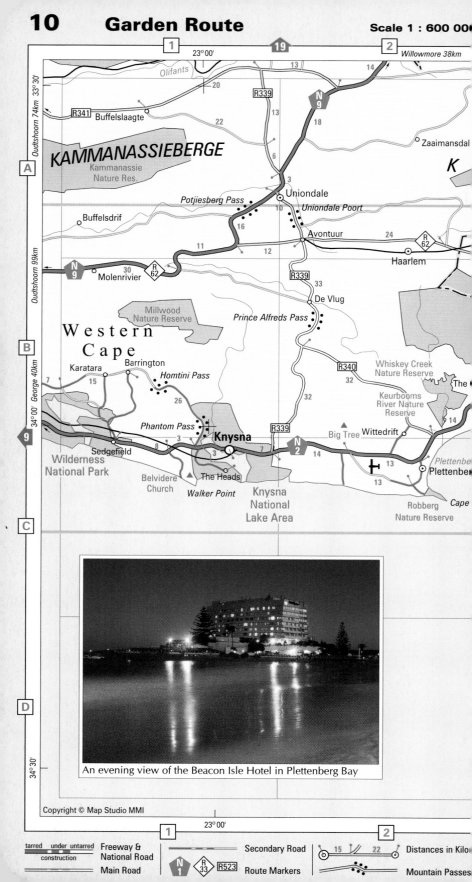

An evening view of the Beacon Isle Hotel in Plettenberg Bay

Copyright © Map Studio MMI

Map labels:

Willowmore 38km

Olifants

R341 Buffelslaagte

20

R339

N9

13

14

13

18

22

6

Zaaimansdal

K

KAMMANASSIEBERGE

Kammanassie Nature Res.

3

Potjiesberg Pass

Uniondale

Uniondale Poort

Buffelsdrif

10

16

11

12

Avontuur

24

R 62

N9   30   R 62

Molenrivier

R339

33

Haarlem

De Vlug

Millwood Nature Reserve

Prince Alfreds Pass

Western Cape

Whiskey Creek Nature Reserve

R340

32

The

Karatara

15

Barrington

Homtini Pass

Keurbooms River Nature Reserve

7

26

32

14

Phantom Pass

3

Knysna

R339

Big Tree

Wittedrift

13

Sedgefield

8

3

7

N2

14

Plettenbe

Plettenber

Wilderness National Park

Belvidere Church

The Heads

Walker Point

Knysna National Lake Area

13

13

Robberg Nature Reserve

Cape

Oudtshoorn 74km   33° 30'

Oudtshoorn 99km

George 40km   34° 00'

9

34° 30'

23° 00'

19

1

2

A

B

C

D

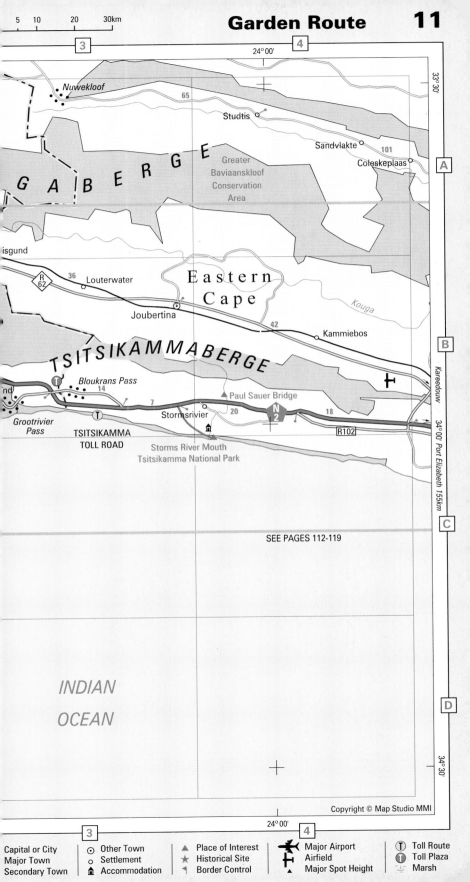

INDIAN

OCEAN

Eastern
Cape

TSITSIKAMMABERGE

GA BERGE

Greater
Baviaanskloof
Conservation
Area

Nuwekloof

Studtis

Sandvlakte

Coleskeplaas

Louterwater

Joubertina

Kammiebos

Kouga

Bloukrans Pass

Grootrivier
Pass

Stormsrivier

Paul Sauer Bridge

TSITSIKAMMA
TOLL ROAD

Storms River Mouth
Tsitsikamma National Park

SEE PAGES 112-119

Kareedouw

Port Elizabeth 155km

R 62

R102

N 2

isgund

nd

36

65

101

42

7

14

20

18

5 10   20   30km

3

4

24° 00'

33° 30'

A

B

C

D

34° 30'

34° 00'

24° 00'

3

4

Capital or City	⊙ Other Town	▲ Place of Interest	✈ Major Airport	Ⓣ Toll Route
Major Town	○ Settlement	★ Historical Site	Airfield	Ⓣ Toll Plaza
Secondary Town	⌂ Accommodation	◄ Border Control	Major Spot Height	Marsh

Scale 1 : 600 000

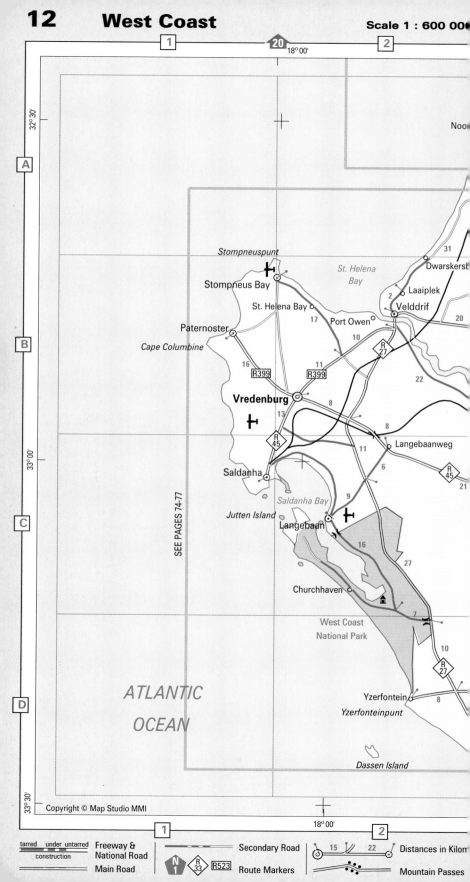

SEE PAGES 74-77

Stompneuspunt

St. Helena Bay

Dwarskers

Stompneus Bay

31

St. Helena Bay

Laaiplek

Velddrif

2

Paternoster

Port Owen

17

10

20

Cape Columbine

16

R399

11

R399

R 27

22

Vredenburg

8

13

R 45

8

Langebaanweg

11

R 45

6

Saldanha

21

9

Saldanha Bay

Jutten Island

Langebaan

16

27

Churchhaven

7

West Coast
National Park

10

R 27

ATLANTIC

Yzerfontein

OCEAN

Yzerfonteinpunt

8

Dassen Island

Noo

32° 30'

18° 00'

20

1

2

A

B

33° 00'

C

D

33° 30'

Copyright © Map Studio MMI

18° 00'

1

2

tarred   under   untarred   **Freeway &**
construction   **National Road**

Main Road

N
1   R 33   R523

Secondary Road

Route Markers

15   22

Distances in Kilom

Mountain Passes

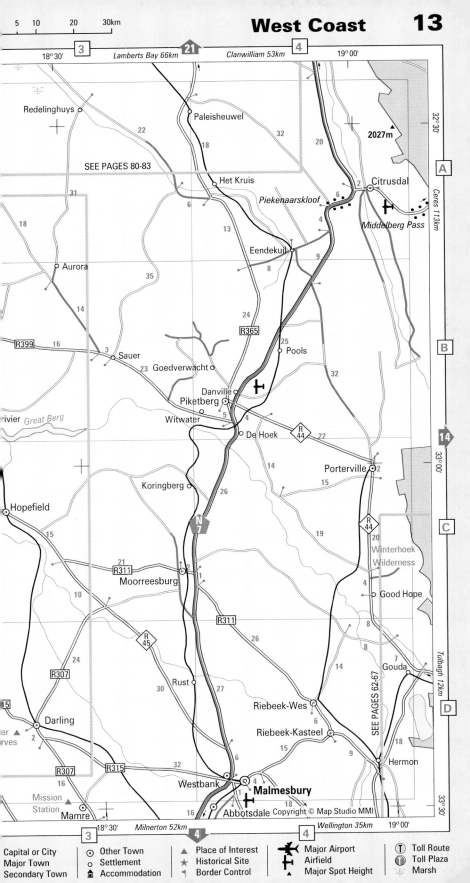

5   10   20   30km

Redelinghuys

Paleisheuwel

22

32

18

20

2027m

A

32° 30'

SEE PAGES 80-83

31

Het Kruis

6

Piekenaarskloof

2

Citrusdal

6

Middelberg Pass

Ceres 113km

18

4

13

Aurora

14

Eendekuil

9

35

8

24

R365

B

R399

16

25

Pools

Sauer

3

Goedverwacht

23

Danville

32

33° 00'

Piketberg

5

Witwater

4

De Hoek

R44

22

14

Porterville

2

Koringberg

15

26

Great Berg

rivier

Hopefield

N7

19

R44

20

Winterhoek Wilderness

C

15

4

Good Hope

21

R311

Moorreesburg

2

1

8

10

R311

14

Gouda

7

R45

26

R307

24

30

Rust

27

Riebeek-Wes

14

SEE PAGES 62-67

Tulbagh 12km

D

15

6

Riebeek-Kasteel

Darling

2

15

9

Hermon

18

R307

R315

32

6

16

Westbank

4

Malmesbury

Mission Station

18

Mamre

16

Abbotsdale Copyright © Map Studio MMI

33° 30'

Capital or City	⊙ Other Town	▲ Place of Interest	✈ Major Airport
Major Town	○ Settlement	★ Historical Site	✈ Airfield
Secondary Town	🏛 Accommodation	◄ Border Control	▲ Major Spot Height

Toll Route

Toll Plaza

Marsh

1   **22** 19° 30'   *Calvinia 107km*   **2**

25

Cederberg
Wilderness

▲ 2027m
• Cedarberg

43

A

Middelberg Pass

Citrusdal 67km

61

67

W e s t e r n
C a p e

B

Bokfontein ○

R303

33

Kromfontein ○

17

13

33° 00'

Groot
Winterhoek
Wilderness
Area

SEE PAGES 62-67

S W A R T R U G G E N S

C

20

▲ 1666m

29

Porterville 40km

▲ Monbijou
Historical
Buildings

Gydo Pass

10

Die V

6

Tulbagh ⊙   ▲ Drostdy

R46

Hottentotskloof ○

14

Prince Alfred
Hamlet ⊙

Gouda ⊙

12

R46

Bella Vista ⊙

30

D

5

10

Nduli ○

Voëlvlei

R46

Ceres ⊙

Malmesbury 46km

15

18

Hawequas
Con. Area

18

Wolseley ⊙

Montana ⊙

Ceres Mtn.
Fynbos
Reserve

H E X R I V E R   M T S.

2251m

Hex River Pass

Tur

15

Michell's Pass

De Doorns ○

33° 30'

19° 00'   **1**   **5**   19° 30'   **2**   *Worcester 36km*

---

tarred	under	untarred	**Freeway &**		**Secondary Road**		15	22	**Distances in Kilo**
	construction		**National Road**						

N   R33   R523   **Main Road**   **Route Markers**   **Mountain Passe**

5 10 20 30km

3 23 4

20° 00' 20° 30'

Bo-Wadrif

26

32° 30'

Tankwa

27

Verlatekloof

A

8

R354

38

N o r t h e r n

90

C a p e

B

16

33° 00'

54

C

32

Beaufort West 256km

27 3 24

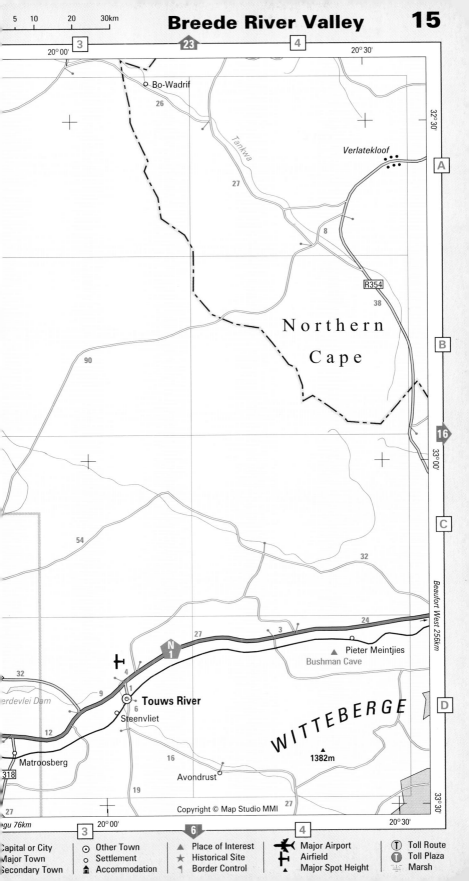

N 1

Pieter Meintjies

Bushman Cave

4

9 1

erdevlei Dam

Touws River

6

Steenvliet

D

W I T T E B E R G E

32

12

1382m

Matroosberg

318

16

Avondrust

19

27

27 Copyright © Map Studio MMI

33° 30'

gu 76km

20° 00' 20° 30'

3 6 4

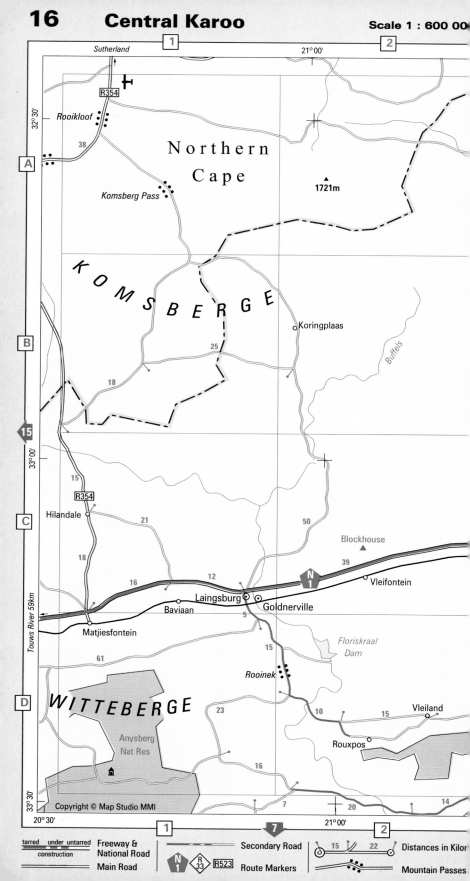

Sutherland

21° 00'

R354

32° 30'

Rooikloof

38

Komsberg Pass

N o r t h e r n
C a p e

▲ 1721m

A

K O M S B E R G E

25

18

B

Koringplaas

Buffels

15

33° 00'

15

R354

Hilandale

21

50

Blockhouse ▲

18

39

C

12

N 1

Vleifontein

16

Laingsburg

Baviaan

Goldnerville

5

Matjiesfontein

Touws River 59km

61

15

Floriskraal Dam

W I T T E B E R G E

Rooinek

23

10

15

Vleiland

D

Anysberg Nat Res

16

Rouxpos

33° 30'

Copyright © Map Studio MMI

7

20

14

20° 30'

21° 00'

tarred under untarred
construction

Freeway &
National Road

Main Road

N 1 R 33 R523

Secondary Road

Route Markers

15   22

Distances in Kilor

Mountain Passes

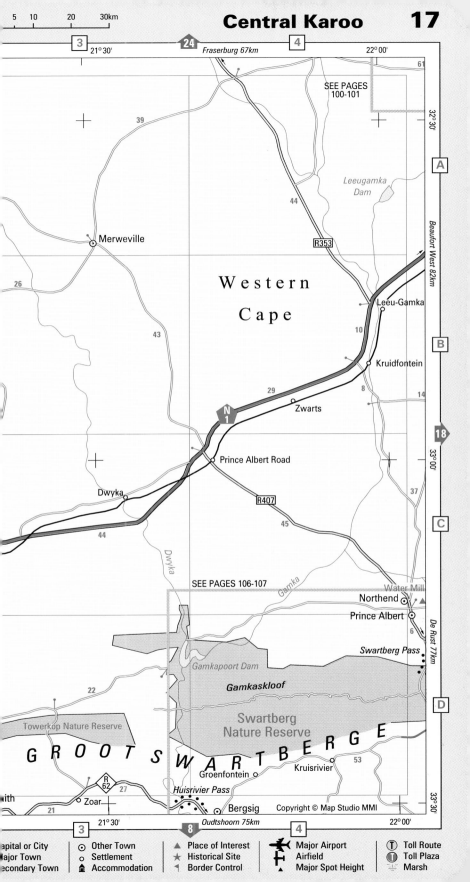

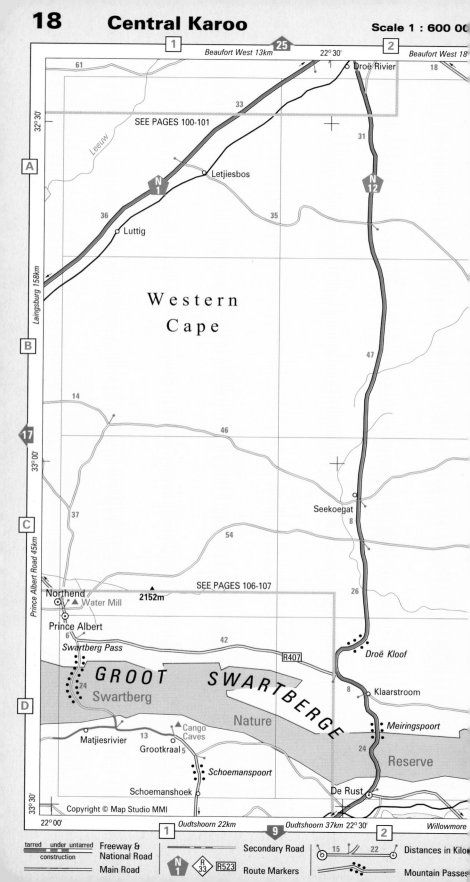

| 1 | 25 | 2 |

Beaufort West 13km   22° 30'   Beaufort West 18

61

o Droë Rivier

18

33

31

SEE PAGES 100-101

32° 30'

A

N1

o Letjiesbos

N12

36

35

o Luttig

W e s t e r n

C a p e

47

B

17

14

46

33° 00'

Prince Albert Road 45km

Laingsburg 158km

C

37

54

Seekoegat

8

SEE PAGES 106-107

26

Northend
▲ Water Mill
2152m

Prince Albert

6

Swartberg Pass

42

R407

Droë Kloof

G R O O T

S W A R T B E R G E

24

Swartberg

8

o Klaarstroom

D

Nature

Meiringspoort

▲ Cango Caves

24

Reserve

Matjiesrivier   13

Grootkraal 5

Schoemanspoort

Schoemanshoek

o De Rust

33° 30'

22° 00'

| 1 | Oudtshoorn 22km | 9 | Oudtshoorn 37km 22° 30' | 2 | Willowmore |

tarred	under	untarred	**Freeway &**			**Secondary Road**		**Distances in Kilom**
construction			**National Road**					
			Main Road	**N1**	R33 R523	**Route Markers**	15 22	**Mountain Passes**

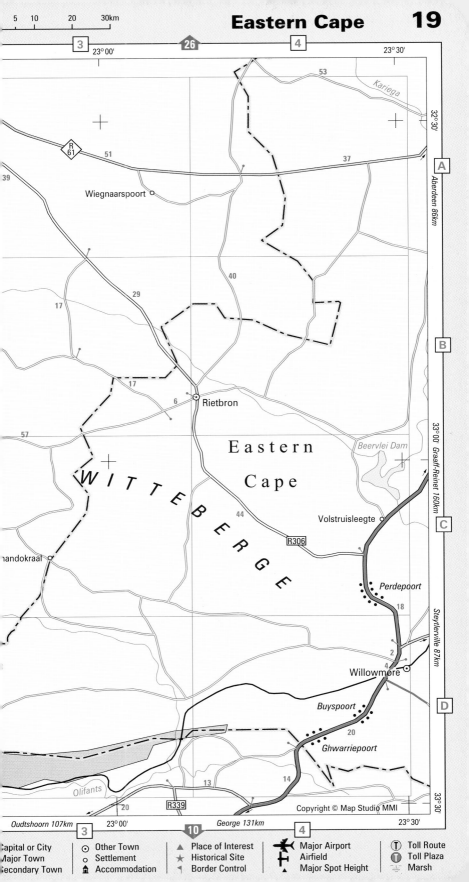

5 10 20 30km

3 26 4

23°00' 23°30'

53

Kariega

32°30'

R61 51 37

A

Aberdeen 86km

39

Wiegnaarspoort

40

29

17

B

17

6 Rietbron

33°00'

57 *Beervlei Dam*

Graaff-Reinet 160km

E a s t e r n

C a p e

44

Volstruisleegte

C

R306

...handokraal

Perdepoort

18

Steytlerville 87km

2

4

Willowmore

D

Buyspoort

20

Ghwarriepoort

13 14

Olifants

20

R339

33°30'

Copyright © Map Studio MMI

Capital or City ⊙ Other Town ▲ Place of Interest ✈ Major Airport Ⓣ Toll Route

Major Town ○ Settlement ★ Historical Site Airfield Ⓣ Toll Plaza

Secondary Town ⌂ Accommodation ◄ Border Control ▲ Major Spot Height Marsh

Stompneus

18° 00'

28

Bitterfontein 64km

2

1

31° 30'

A

24

Koekenaap

Lutzvi

7

Cliff Point

26

27

R362

Papendorp

B

Strandfontein

7

Doring Bay

19

Cape Donkin

The Maltese Cross in the Cederberg   See Page 22

Bird Island ▲

Lamberts Bay ◉

C

32° 00'

Wadrifmond

SEE PAGES 80-83

ATLANTIC

OCEAN

Elands

D

Baboon Point

18° 00'

1

12

2

tarred   under   untarred   **Freeway &**   Secondary Road   ◉ 15 / 22 ◉   Distances in Kilo

construction   **National Road**

   N 1   R 33   R523   Route Markers   Mountain Passe

Main Road

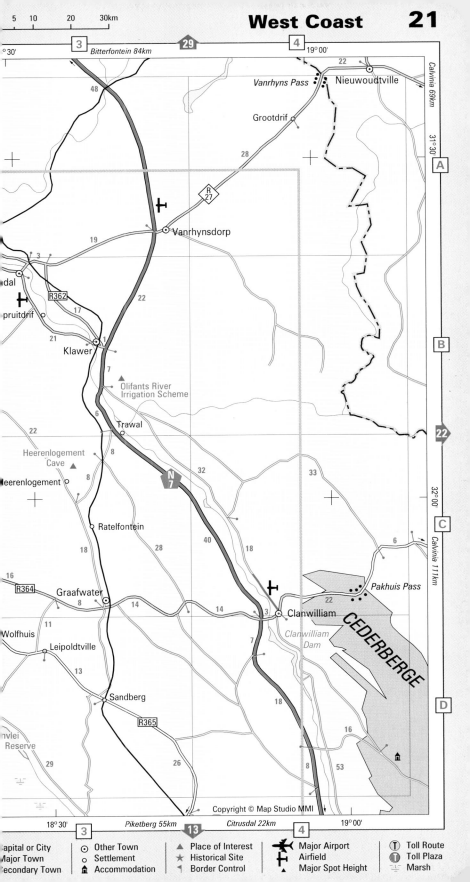

5 10 20 30km

°30'
31° 30'
A
22 Nieuwoudtville
Vanrhyns Pass
Grootdrif
28
R 27
Vanrhynsdorp
19
3
dal
R362
pruitdrif 17
21
Klawer B
7
Olifants River
Irrigation Scheme
6
Trawal 22
22
8
Heerenlogement
Cave
8 N 7
eerenlogement 8 32 33
Ratelfontein C
18 28 40 18
16
R364
Graafwater 6 Pakhuis Pass
8 14 14 3 Clanwilliam 22
Wolfhuis
11 Clanwilliam CEDERBERGE
Leipoldtville Dam
13 7
18
Sandberg
R365
16
nvlei
Reserve 26 53
29 8
D

Calvinia 69km
32° 00'
22
Calvinia 111km

apital or City   Other Town   ▲ Place of Interest   ✈ Major Airport   Ⓣ Toll Route
Major Town   ∘ Settlement   ★ Historical Site   ✈ Airfield   Ⓣ Toll Plaza
econdary Town   🏛 Accommodation   ◤ Border Control   ▲ Major Spot Height   Marsh

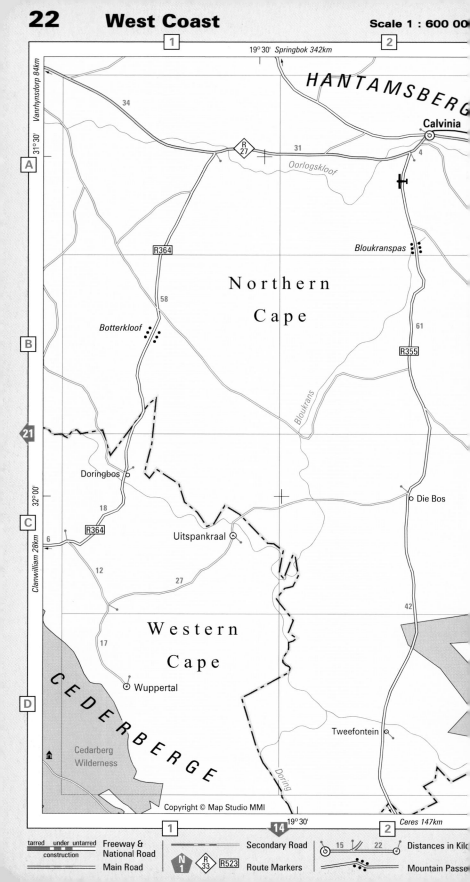

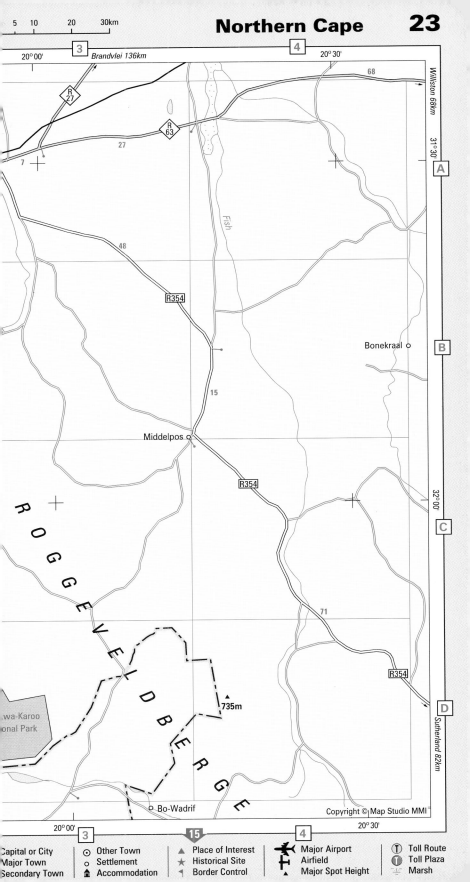

5 10 20 30km

20°00' *Brandvlei 136km* 20°30'

68

Williston 68km

R27

R63

27

31°30'

A

7

Fish

48

R354

Bonekraal ○

B

15

Middelpos ○

R354

32°00'

C

71

R354

Sutherland 82km

D

R O G G E V E L D B E R G E

▲ 735m

...wa-Karoo ...onal Park

○ Bo-Wadrif

20°00' 20°30'

Capital or City   ⊙ Other Town   ▲ Place of Interest   ✈ Major Airport   Ⓣ Toll Route
Major Town   ○ Settlement   ★ Historical Site   ⊥ Airfield   Ⓣ Toll Plaza
Secondary Town   🏠 Accommodation   ◀ Border Control   ▲ Major Spot Height   Marsh

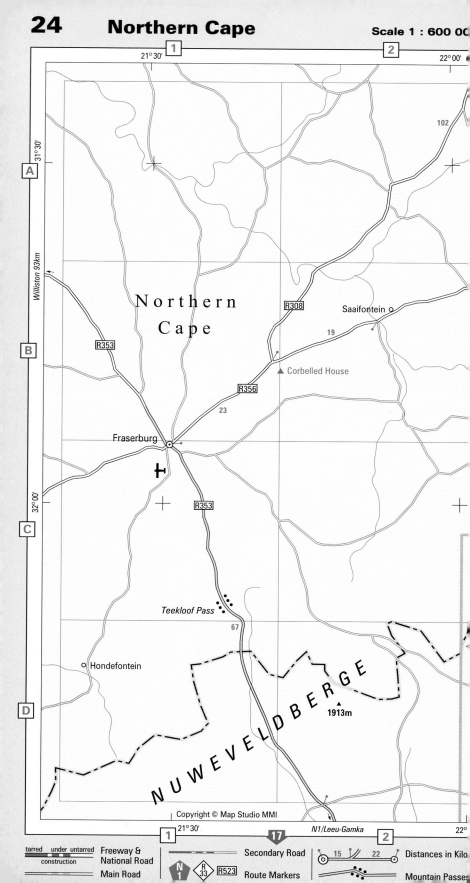

Northern Cape

Fraserburg

Saaifontein

Corbelled House

R308

R356

R353

R353

Teekloof Pass

Hondefontein

NUWEVELDBERGE

▲ 1913m

Williston 93km

N1/Leeu-Gamka

Copyright © Map Studio MMI

tarred   under   untarred
construction   Freeway &
National Road
Main Road   Secondary Road   Distances in Kilo

N1   R33   R523   Route Markers   Mountain Passes

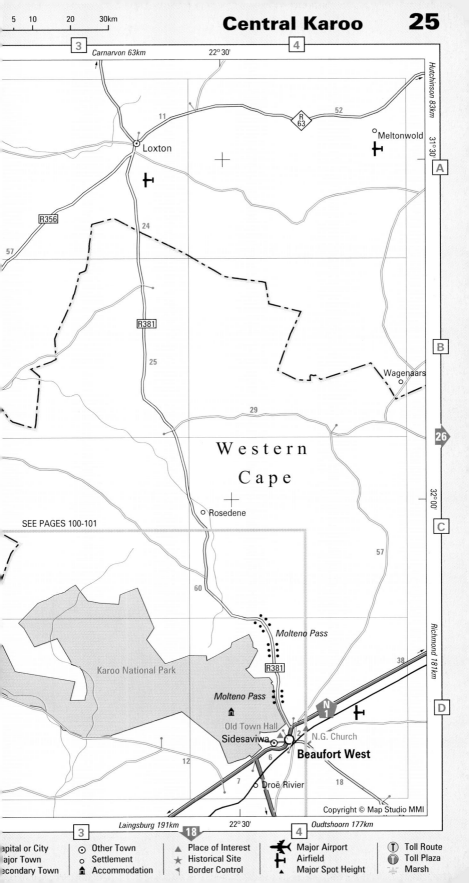

5 10 20 30km

3 Carnarvon 63km 22° 30' 4

Hutchinson 83km

11 R 63 52

Meltonwold

Loxton 31° 30' A

R356

57 24

R381

25 B

Wagenaars

26

29 32° 00'

W e s t e r n

C a p e C

Rosedene

SEE PAGES 100-101

57

60

Karoo National Park Molteno Pass

R381 38

Molteno Pass Richmond 181km

Old Town Hall N1 D

Sidesaviwa N.G. Church

Beaufort West

12 2

6

7 Droë Rivier 18

Copyright © Map Studio MMI

Laingsburg 191km 18 22° 30' 4 Oudtshoorn 177km

3

apital or City | ⊙ Other Town | ▲ Place of Interest | ✈ Major Airport | Ⓣ Toll Route
ajor Town | ○ Settlement | ★ Historical Site | Airfield | Ⓣ Toll Plaza
econdary Town | 🏛 Accommodation | ◄ Border Control | ▲ Major Spot Height | Marsh

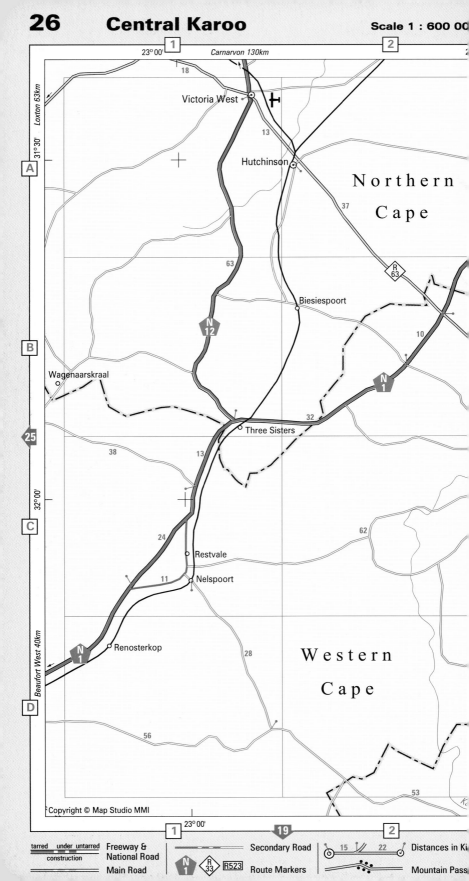

23° 00'
Carnarvon 130km
Loxton 63km
31°30'

Victoria West
18
13
Hutchinson

N o r t h e r n

C a p e

37
R 63
63
10
N 12
Biesiespoort
N 1

Wagenaarskraal
25
32
Three Sisters
38
13

32° 00'

24
Restvale
62
11
Nelspoort

N 1
Renosterkop
28

W e s t e r n

C a p e

Beaufort West 40km

56
53

Copyright © Map Studio MMI

23° 00'
19
15
22
Distances in Ki

tarred under untarred
construction
Freeway &
National Road
Secondary Road
N 1 R 33 R523 Route Markers
Main Road
Mountain Pass

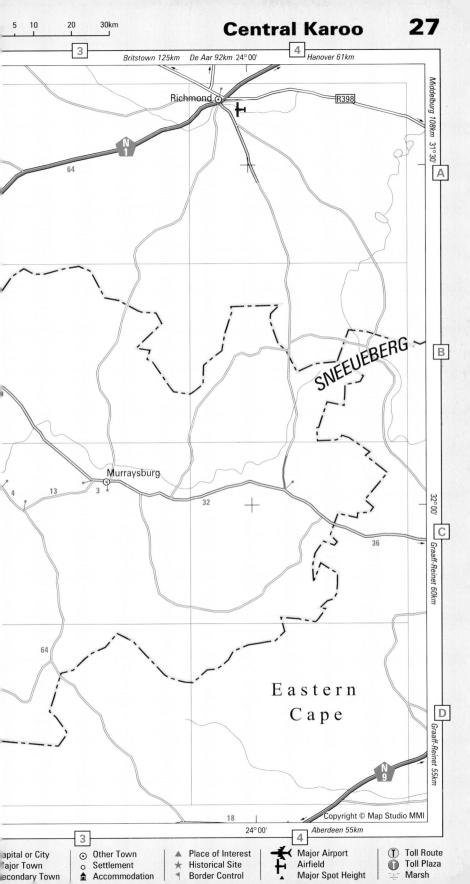

Britstown 125km **De Aar 92km** 24° 00' **Hanover 61km**

Richmond

R398

Middelburg 108km

N1

64

A

SNEEUEBERG

B

Murraysburg

4   13   3   32

C

36

32° 00'

Graaff-Reinet 60km

64

E a s t e r n
C a p e

D

Graaff-Reinet 55km

N9

18

24° 00'   **Aberdeen 55km**

apital or City	⊙ Other Town
ajor Town	∘ Settlement
econdary Town	⌂ Accommodation

▲ Place of Interest	
★ Historical Site	
◀ Border Control	

✈ Major Airport	T Toll Route
Airfield	T Toll Plaza
▲ Major Spot Height	Marsh

Springbok 114km

18° 00'

Kamiesberg

Platba

Spoegrivier

Witwater

Karkams

114

30° 30'

A

Garies

12

B

Swartdoring

46

R358

N
7

Kotzesrus

Rietpoort

5

Biesiesfontein

31° 00'

C

4

Bitterfontein

16

Nuwerus

Komkans

Klein-Goerap

R363

W e s t e r n

28

D

C a p e

Blinkwater Bay

Landplaas

Stompneus

18° 00'

20

Vredendal 51km

tarred   under   untarred
construction

**Freeway &
National Road**

Main Road

Secondary Road

15

22

Distances in Kilo

N
1

R
33

R523

Route Markers

Mountain Passe

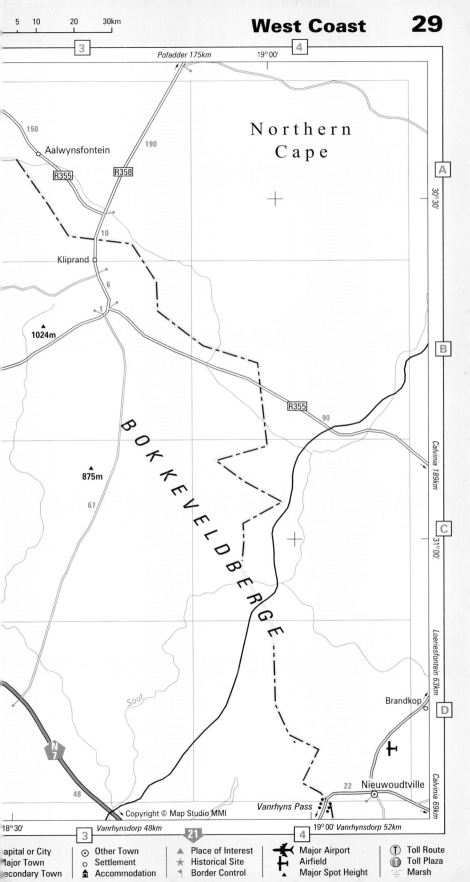

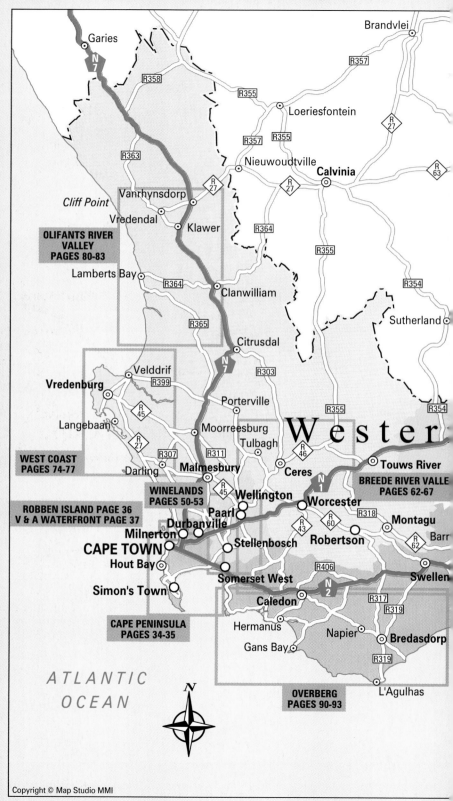

Brandvlei

Garies

R357

R358

R355

Loeriesfontein

R357 R355

R
27

R363

Nieuwoudtville

Calvinia

R
27

R
63

Vanrhynsdorp

Cliff Point

Vredendal

Klawer

R364

R
27

**OLIFANTS RIVER
VALLEY
PAGES 80-83**

R355

Lamberts Bay

R364

Clanwilliam

R354

Sutherland

R365

Citrusdal

N
7

R303

Wester

Velddrif

R399

R355

R354

Vredenburg

Porterville

R
45

Langebaan

Moorreesburg

R
46

Touws River

R
27

R307

Tulbagh

**BREEDE RIVER VALLE
PAGES 62-67**

**WEST COAST
PAGES 74-77**

R311

N
1

Darling

Malmesbury

Ceres

Worcester

**WINELANDS
PAGES 50-53**

R
45

Wellington

R318

Montagu

**ROBBEN ISLAND PAGE 36
V & A WATERFRONT PAGE 37**

Paarl

R
43

R
60

Robertson

R
62

Barr

Durbanville

Milnerton

CAPE TOWN

Stellenbosch

Hout Bay

R406

Swellen

Simon's Town

Somerset West

N
2

R317

Caledon

R319

**CAPE PENINSULA
PAGES 34-35**

Hermanus

Napier

Bredasdorp

Gans Bay

R319

ATLANTIC

OCEAN

N

L'Agulhas

**OVERBERG
PAGES 90-93**

Copyright © Map Studio MMI

Cape Metropolitan Area   Winelands   Breede River Valley   West

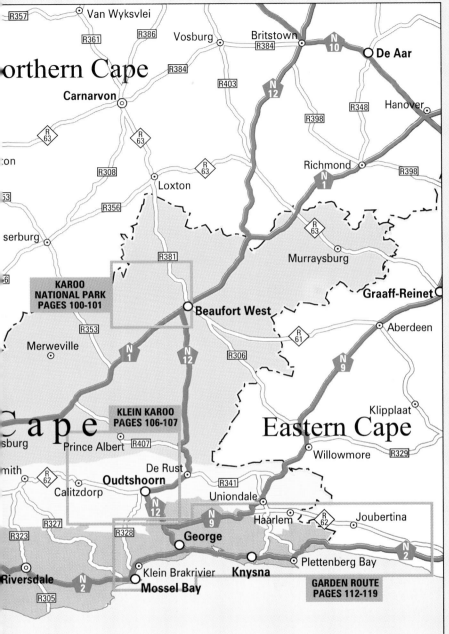

A range of jagged mountains thrusting into the splendid desolation of the southern Atlantic, the Cape Peninsula is one of the world's most beautiful places. Cape Town, the South Peninsula, Blaauwberg, Helderberg, Tygerberg and Oostenberg form Greater Cape Town, a large and verdant expanse stretching from the foot of Table Mountain to the Hottentots Holland range in the purple distance. Sandy shores, mountain peaks, wildlife parks, forests and dunes permeate this diverse southern wonder-world, which has enticed visitors since the first seafarers sailed into Table Bay and coined the descriptive phrase the fairest cape in the whole circumference of the earth.

With a bustling, cosmopolitan city life alongside its spectacular scenery, Greater Cape Town's six regions offer everything the discerning visitor could wish for.

The South Peninsula, home to the Cape Peninsula National Park, is a dazzling showcase of the area's indigenous flora and fauna. Cape Town, the cosmopolitan hub of the area, was voted third in a recent international poll of top tourist destinations – and for good reason. Its pristine beaches are a stone's throw from the pulse of the Victoria and Alfred Waterfront, where upmarket shopping malls, arts and crafts markets, theatres and live

music uniquely meld with the surrounding working harbour. Museums and art galleries abound and South Africa's oldest building, the Castle of Good Hope, is in the city centre – not far from the cobbled streets of the Bo-Kaap with their delightful old buildings.

THE CLASSIC VIEW OF TABLE MOUNTAIN FROM BLOUBERG

The Blaauwberg region, which boasts the best views of Table Mountain, South Africa's most famous landmark, is a favourite of windsurfers and kite-flyers alike. Ratanga Junction, the wildest theme park in Africa, is also situated in this region. Tygerberg has both a commercial and residential area as well as fertile farmlands, while Oostenberg is home to sweeping vistas of undulating vineyards. The beautiful Helderberg is the sixth region, offering unsurpassed whale-watching vantage points and a myriad scenic mountain walks.

The Cape
South Africa
Western Cape Tourism Board
www.capetourism.org

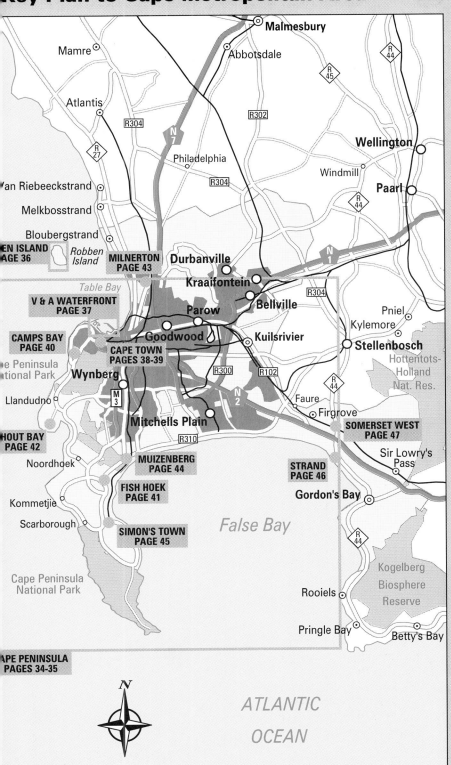

Malmesbury

Mamre

Abbotsdale

R45

R44

Atlantis

R302

R304

N7

Wellington

R27

Philadelphia

Windmill

R304

Paarl

van Riebeeckstrand

R44

Melkbosstrand

Bloubergstrand

EN ISLAND AGE 36

Robben Island

Table Bay

MILNERTON PAGE 43

Durbanville

Kraaifontein

V & A WATERFRONT PAGE 37

Parow

Bellville

R304

Pniel

Kylemore

CAMPS BAY PAGE 40

Goodwood

Kuilsrivier

Stellenbosch

e Peninsula tional Park

CAPE TOWN PAGES 38-39

Hottentots-Holland Nat. Res.

Wynberg

R300

R102

R44

Llandudno

M3

N2

Faure

Firgrove

HOUT BAY PAGE 42

Mitchells Plain

SOMERSET WEST PAGE 47

Noordhoek

R310

Sir Lowry's Pass

MUIZENBERG PAGE 44

STRAND PAGE 46

Kommetjie

FISH HOEK PAGE 41

Gordon's Bay

Scarborough

False Bay

SIMON'S TOWN PAGE 45

R44

Cape Peninsula National Park

Kogelberg Biosphere Reserve

Rooiels

APE PENINSULA PAGES 34-35

Pringle Bay

Betty's Bay

N

ATLANTIC

OCEAN

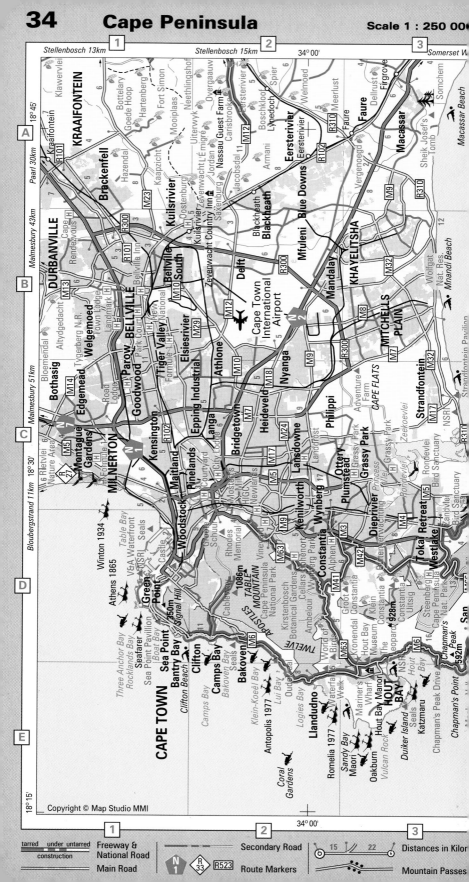

tarred under untarred
construction

Freeway &
National Road

Main Road

Secondary Road

Route Markers

Distances in Kilometres

Mountain Passes

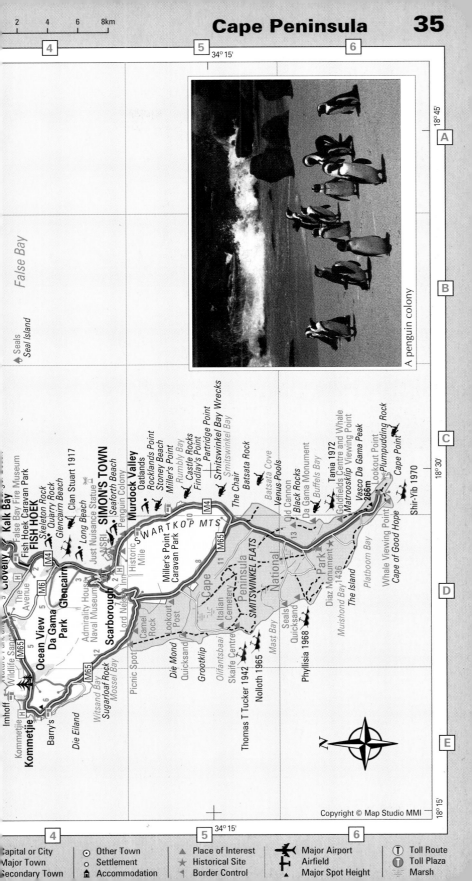

A penguin colony

2 4 6 8km

34° 15'

18° 45'

18° 30'

18° 15'

34° 15'

False Bay

▲ Seals
Seal Island

Kalk Bay
False Bay Fire Museum
FISH HOEK
Fish Hoek Caravan Park
Skeleton Rock
Quarry Rock
Clan Stuart 1917
Glencairn Beach
SIMON'S TOWN
Long Beach
Just Nuisance Statue
Admiralty House
Naval Museum
Penguin Colony
Seaforth Beach
Murdock Valley
Oatlands
Rocklands Point
Stoney Beach
Miller's Point
Rumbly Bay
Castle Rocks
Findlay's Point
Partridge Point
Smitswinkel Bay Wrecks
Smitswinkel Bay
The Chair
Batsata Rock
Batsata Cove
Venus Pools
Old Cannon
Black Rocks
Da Gama Monument
Buffels Bay
Tania 1972
Goldfields Centre and Whale
Matrooskip Viewing Point
Vasco Da Gama Peak 266m
Lookout Point
Plumpudding Rock
Cape Point
Shir-Yib 1970

Clovelly
The Avenue
Glencairn
Ocean View
Da Gama Park
Scarborough
Lord Nelson Inn
Historic Mile
Miller's Point Caravan Park
S W A R T K O P   M T S
Cape
Peninsula
SMITSWINKEL FLATS
National
Park
Italian Cemetery
Seals
Quicksand
Phyllisia 1968
Mast Bay
Diaz Monument
Muishond Bay 143m
The Island
Platboom Bay
Whale Viewing Point
Cape of Good Hope
Diaz Monument

Imhoff
Ocean View
Da Gama Park
Barry's
Die Eiland
Kommetjie
Witsand Bay
Mossel Bay
Sugarloaf Rock
Picnic Spot
Camel Rock
Lookout Post
Die Mond
Quicksand
Grootklip
Olifantsbaai
Skaife Centre
Nolloth 1965
Thomas T Tucker 1942

M4 M6 M65 M4 M65

N

Copyright © Map Studio MMI

Capital or City
Major Town
Secondary Town
⊙ Other Town
○ Settlement
🏠 Accommodation
▲ Place of Interest
★ Historical Site
◄ Border Control
✈ Major Airport
Airfield
◄ Major Spot Height
Ⓣ Toll Route
Ⓣ Toll Plaza
Marsh

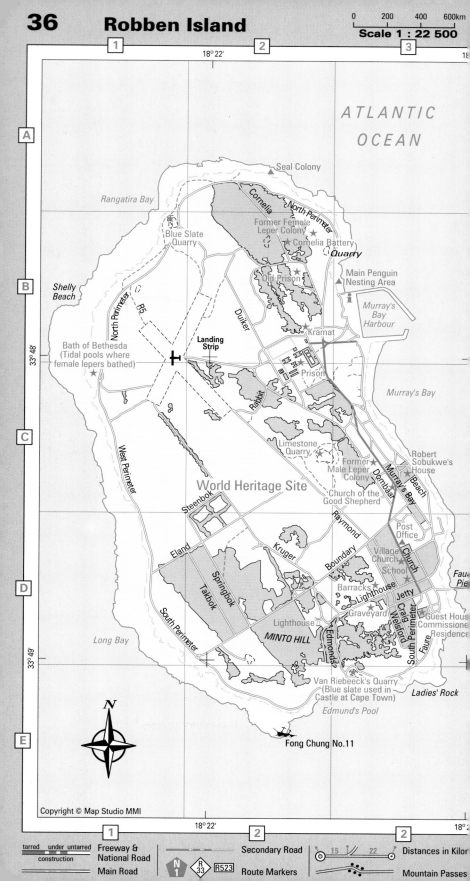

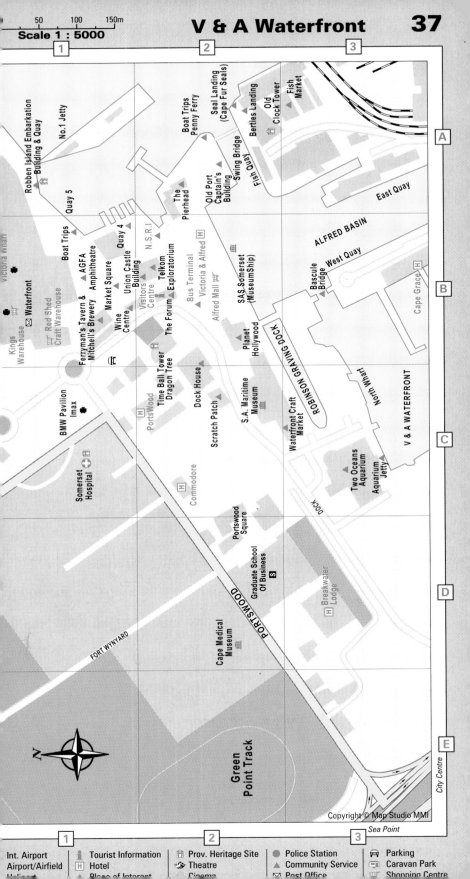

A

B

C

D

E

Robben Island Embarkation
Building & Quay

No.1 Jetty

Boat Trips
Penny Ferry

Seal Landing
(Cape Fur Seals)

Berties Landing

Old
Clock Tower

Fish
Market

Quay 5

The
Pierhead

Old Port
Captain's
Building

Swing Bridge

Fish Quay

East Quay

Boat Trips

AGFA

Amphitheatre

Market Square

Quay 4

Union Castle
Building

N.S.R.I.

Telkom

The
Forum

Exploratorium

Victoria & Alfred

ALFRED BASIN

West Quay

Bascule
Bridge

Cape Grace

Victoria Wharf

Waterfront

Kings
Warehouse

Red Shed
Craft Warehouse

Ferryman's Tavern &
Mitchell's Brewery

Wine
Centre

Visitors
Centre

Bus Terminal

Alfred Mall

SAS Somerset
(MuseumShip)

Planet
Hollywood

ROBINSON GRAVING DOCK

North Wharf

V & A WATERFRONT

BMW Pavilion
Imax

PortsWood

Time Ball Tower
Dragon Tree

Dock House

Scratch Patch

S.A. Maritime
Museum

Waterfront Craft
Market

Somerset
Hospital

Commodore

DOCK

Two Oceans
Aquarium

Aquarium
Jetty

Portswood
Square

Breakwater
Lodge

FORT WYNYARD

Graduate School
Of Business

PORTSWOOD

Cape Medical
Museum

Green
Point Track

N

City Centre

Sea Point

Copyright © Map Studio MMI

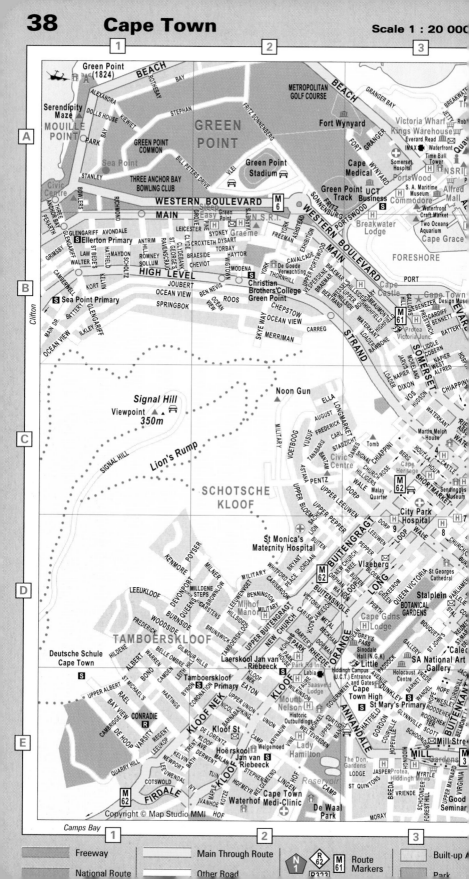

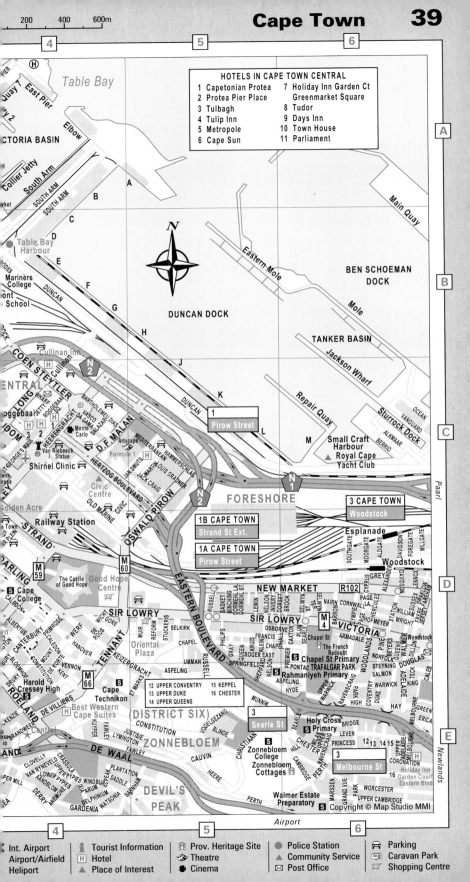

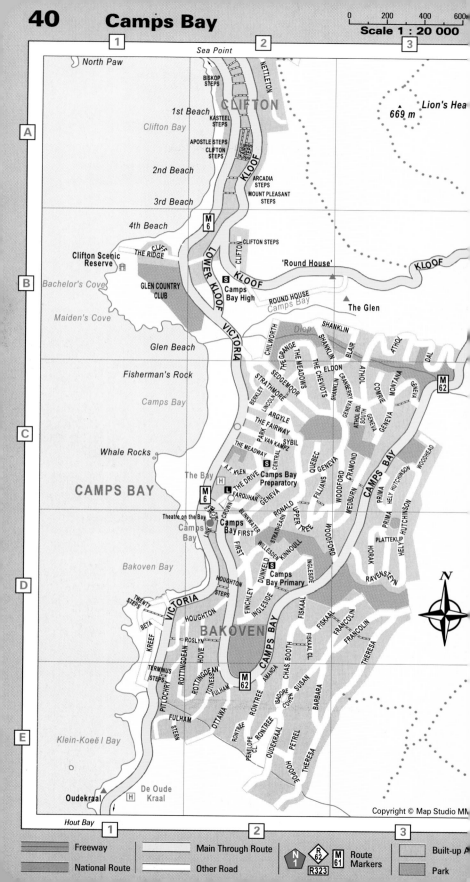

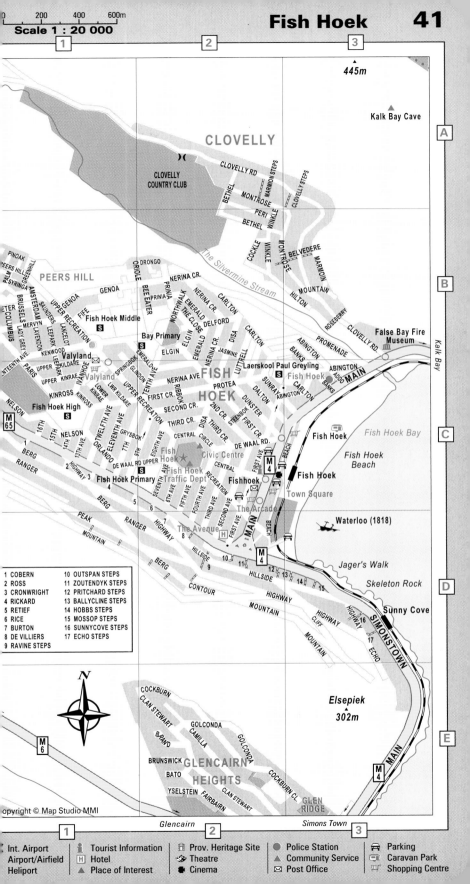

Scale 1 : 20 000

200 400 600m

1 | **2** | **3**

445m

Kalk Bay Cave

A

CLOVELLY

CLOVELLY
COUNTRY CLUB

CLOVELLY RD

BETHEL
MONTROSE
MARMION STEPS
PERI
WINKLE
BETHEL

COCKLE
WINKLE
MONTROSE

BELVEDERE

MARMION

The Silvermine Stream

MOUNTAIN
HILTON

ROSEBERRY

PROMENADE
CLOVELLY RD.

False Bay Fire
Museum

B

PINOAK
PEERS HILL
PEERS HILLS
SYRINGA
PALM

PEERS HILL

AMSTERDAM

DRONGO
ORIOLE
BEE EATER
GENOA
GENOA
FIFE
UPPER RECREATION

PRINIA
NERINA CR.
NORTHWALK
THE CLOSE
EMERALD
DELFORD
CARLTON

Fish Hoek Middle
S

Bay Primary

CARLTON

ABINGTON

KENWOOD
LADY GREY
PARIS
SIXTEENTH AVE
COLUMBUS
BRUSSELS
MERVYN
LAVENDON
SAUNDERS
LEPARK
LANCELO
UPPER GENOA

NERINA CR.
ELGIN
JASMINE
ELGIN
DISA
NERINA AVE
NERINA CR.
EMERALD

BANKS
SUNRAY
BANKS

Laerskool Paul Greyling
Fish Hoek

ABINGTON

MAIN

Valyland
KILDARE
UPPER KINRAE
VANROSS
KINROSS

Valyland
LWR KILDARE
SPRINGBOK
GUNOON
LOWER KINRAE
UPPER RECREATION
TENTH AVE

RIBBON
NERINA AVE
FIRST CR.
SECOND CR.

FISH
HOEK

PROTEA

DALTON
STEENBOK
DUNSTER
FIRST CR.

CARLTON
ABINGTON

Fish Hoek

C

NELSON
M
65

Fish Hoek High
S

16TH
15TH
14TH AVE
NELSON
13TH
ORLANDO
DE WAAL RD UPPER

GRYSBOK
ELEVENTH AVE
TWELFTH AVE

THIRD CR.
DISA
2ND CR.
THIRD CR.
CENTRAL
CIRCLE
DE WAAL RD.

2ND CR.
FIRST CR.

Fish Hoek
Civic Centre

Fish Hoek
Beach

Fish Hoek Bay

Fish Hoek

BERG
RANGER

1

2 Highway 3

Fish Hoek Primary
S

Fishhoek
Fish Hoek
Traffic Dept

RECREATION
NINTH AVE
SEVENTH AVE
6TH AVE
FIFTH AVE
FOURTH AVE
THIRD AVE
SECOND AVE
FIRST AVE

CENTRAL

M
4

Fish Hoek

PEAK
MOUNTAIN

BERG
RANGER

Highway

5

6

The Arcade

Town Square

Waterloo (1818)

D

1 COBERN
2 ROSS
3 CRONWRIGHT
4 RICKARD
5 RETIEF
6 RICE
7 BURTON
8 DE VILLIERS
9 RAVINE STEPS

10 OUTSPAN STEPS
11 ZOUTENDYK STEPS
12 PRITCHARD STEPS
13 BALLYCLINE STEPS
14 HOBBS STEPS
15 MOSSOP STEPS
16 SUNNYCOVE STEPS
17 ECHO STEPS

The Avenue

H

HILLSIDE

CONTOUR

10
9
11
11

HILLSIDE

12 13
14

HIGHWAY
MOUNTAIN

HIGHWAY
CLIFF

MOUNTAIN

15

HIGHWAY
HIGHWAY

Jager's Walk

Skeleton Rock

Sunny Cove

SIMONSTOWN

16

17
ECHO
MAIN

E

N

COCKBURN
CLAN STEWART
BRAND

GOLCONDA
CAMILLA

GOLCONDA

BRUNSWICK
BATO
GLENCAIRN
HEIGHTS
YSELSTEIN FAIRBAIRN

CLAN STEWART
COCKBURN CL.

GLEN
RIDGE

Elsepiek
302m

MAIN
M
4

M
6

opyright © Map Studio MMI

Glencairn | Simons Town

1 | **2** | **3**

Kalk Bay

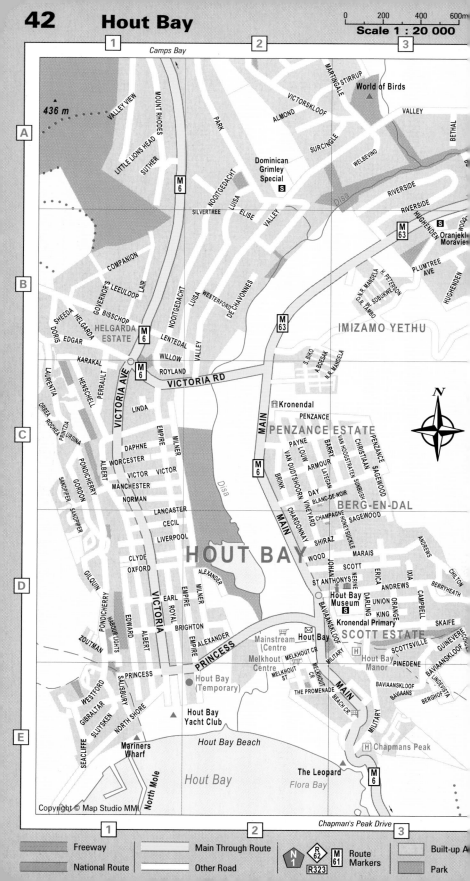

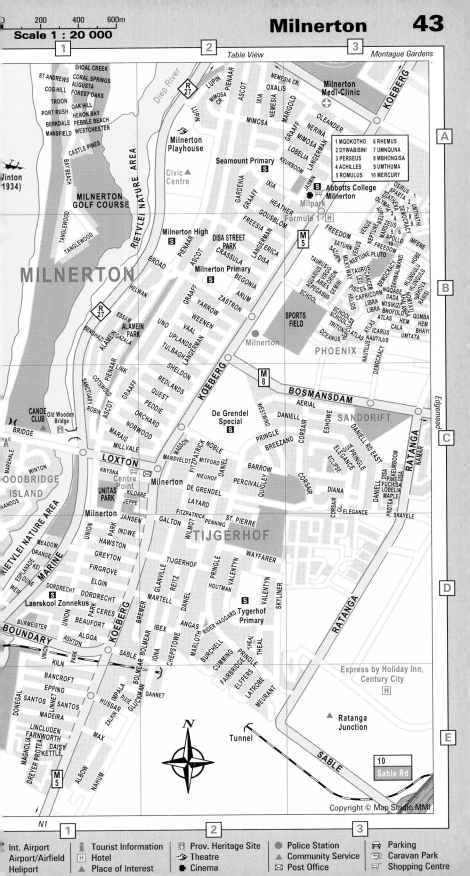

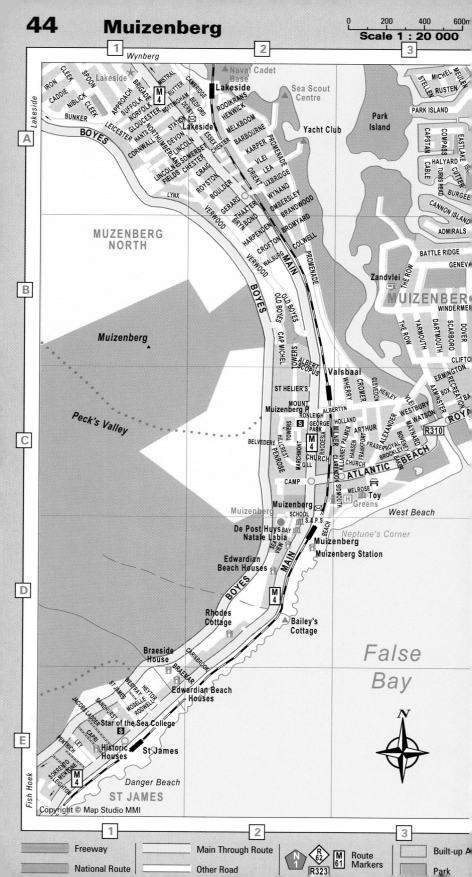

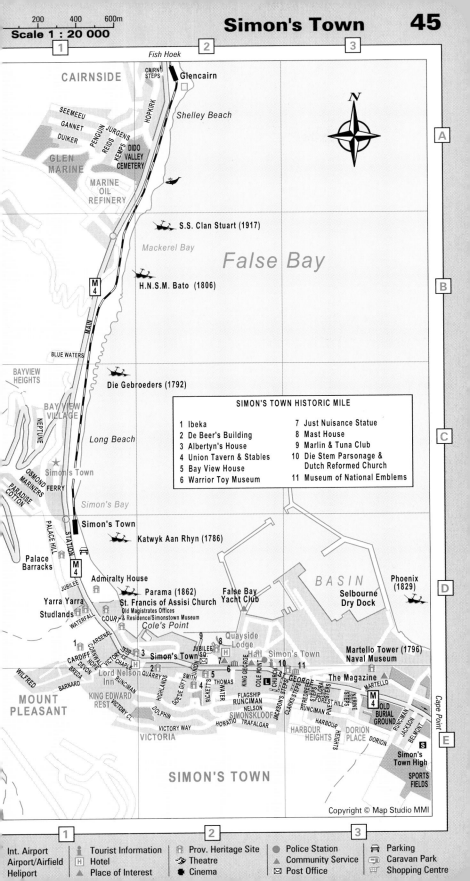

Scale 1 : 20 000
200 400 600m

False Bay

SIMON'S TOWN HISTORIC MILE

1 Ibeka
2 De Beer's Building
3 Albertyn's House
4 Union Tavern & Stables
5 Bay View House
6 Warrior Toy Museum
7 Just Nuisance Statue
8 Mast House
9 Marlin & Tuna Club
10 Die Stem Parsonage & Dutch Reformed Church
11 Museum of National Emblems

CAIRNSIDE
Glencairn
Fish Hoek
Shelley Beach
CAIRN STEPS
HOPKIRK
SEEMEEU
GANNET
DUIKER
PENGUIN
JURGENS
REIDS
KEMPS
DIDO VALLEY CEMETERY
GLEN MARINE
MARINE OIL REFINERY

S.S. Clan Stuart (1917)
Mackerel Bay
H.N.S.M. Bato (1806)

BLUE WATERS
MAIN

BAYVIEW HEIGHTS
BAY VIEW VILLAGE
NEPTUNE
Die Gebroeders (1792)
Long Beach

MARINERS
Simon's Town
OSMOND
FERRY
PARADISE
COTTON
PALACE HILL
STATION
JUBILEE
Palace Barracks

Simon's Town
Katwyk Aan Rhyn (1786)
Simon's Bay

Admiralty House
Parama (1862)
St. Francis of Assisi Church
Old Magistrates Offices
COURT & Residence/Simonstown Museum
Cole's Point

Yarra Yarra
Studlands
WATERFALL

False Bay Yacht Club
Quayside Lodge
JUBILEE SQ.
Simon's Town
Hall
Simon's Town

BASIN
Selbourne Dry Dock
Phoenix (1829)

Martello Tower (1796)
Naval Museum
The Magazine
MARTELLO

MOUNT PLEASANT
WILFRED
CARDIFF
CORNWALL
HOPE
DEVON
BREDA
BARNARD
ARSENAL
319
VICTORY CL.
CHAPEL
Lord Nelson Inn
QUARRY
HIGHLANDS
GOEDE GIFT
RICKETT'S
SMITH
THOMAS
WATER
KING EDWARD REST
RUNCIMAN
DOLPHIN
VICTORY WAY
HORATIO
TRAFALGAR
NELSON
SIMONSKLOOF
FLAGSHIP
RUNCIMAN
KING GEORGE
COLE POINT
JACKSON'S STEPS
ST. GEORGE
CLARK'S STEPS
L CHURCH
FREDREKE
FLORAL
FORREST
NEERIE STEPS
STEPS
FOREST HILLS
RUNCIMAN
HARBOUR
HARBOUR HEIGHTS
DORION PLACE
DORION
RUNCIMAN
JACKSON
BELMONT
OLD BURIAL GROUND
M4

VICTORIA
SIMON'S TOWN

Simon's Town High
SPORTS FIELDS
Cape Point

Copyright © Map Studio MMI

Int. Airport
Airport/Airfield
Heliport
Tourist Information
Hotel
Place of Interest
Prov. Heritage Site
Theatre
Cinema
Police Station
Community Service
Post Office
Parking
Caravan Park
Shopping Centre

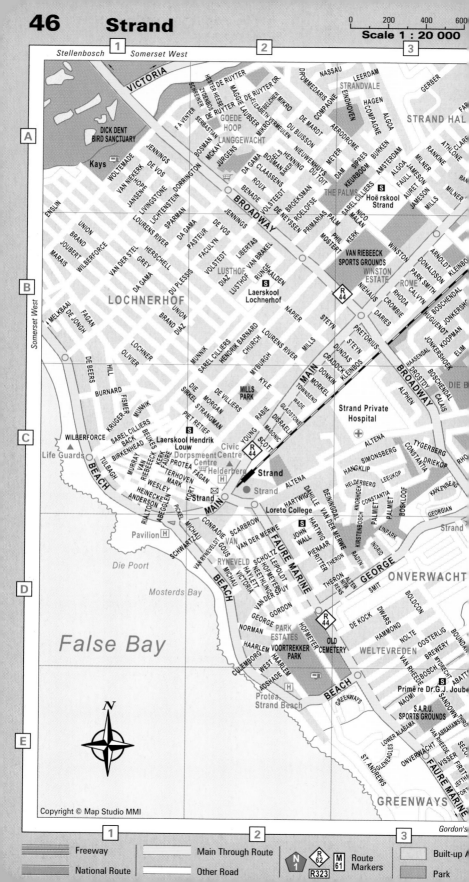

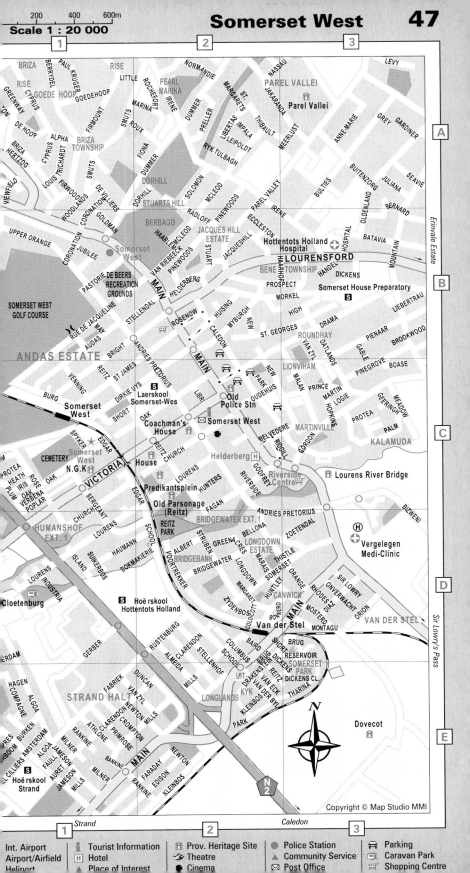

Whether it is its magnificent natural beauty, its rich cultural heritage or its world-renowned wines, the Winelands Region is synonymous with all the best that the Cape has to offer. A 45-minute drive from Cape Town brings you to this area where splendid mountains form a dramatic backdrop to lush vineyards and gabled Cape Dutch homesteads steeped in history. Come experience the hospitality and beauty of Stellenbosch, Paarl, Wellington and Franschhoek. The diversity of the Winelands will capture every heart.

Follow in the footsteps of our ancestors as you stroll along the oak-lined streets of Stellenbosch, the second oldest town in the country. Our colourful history comes to life in the splendidly restored Cape Dutch, Georgian and Victorian buildings in each town. Monuments such as the Huguenot Memorial and Afrikaans Language Monument and the many outstanding museums provide a fascinating glimpse into the past.

DRYING FRUIT IN THE HOT SUMMER SUN

The excellent wines produced in this area are world-renowned. You will be spoilt for choice between small, boutique wineries and the larger, more commercial wine estates. Taste the fruit of the vintner's labour in the magnificent surrounds that are so characteristic of the Winelands, or join the winemaker on a tour of his cellar where the precious harvest is lovingly transformed into every wine lover's delight. To revive fatigued taste buds, the Winelands boast some of the finest restaurants in the Cape, offering from traditional fare to the more exotic. And don't miss out on other culinary delights produced in the region such as cheese, olives, herbs, berries and much more.

With its rugged mountains and fertile valleys, the Winelands is paradise to nature lovers and outdoor enthusiasts. Invigorating hikes through the many nature reserves in the area will have you marvelling at the indigenous Fynbos that flourishes here. Whether you enjoy the thrill of tearing down the hillside on a mountain bike, or relaxing next to a tranquil river catching trout, the exhilaration of a hot-air balloon-ride over the granite outcrops of Paarl Mountain or savouring the beauty of the setting sun on horseback, the Winelands will surpass your every expectation.

theCape
South Africa
Western Cape Tourism Board
www.capetourism.org

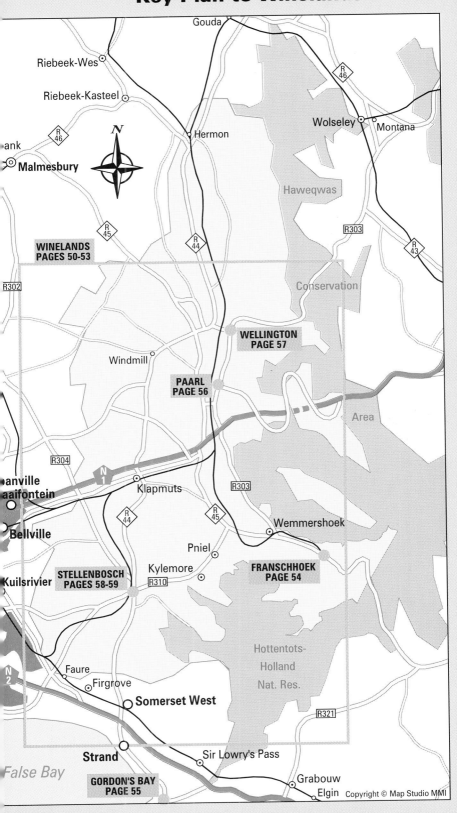

Gouda

Riebeek-Wes

Riebeek-Kasteel

R 46

ank

Malmesbury

N

Hermon

Wolseley

Montana

R 46

Haweqwas

R 45

R 44

R303

R 43

WINELANDS PAGES 50-53

R302

Conservation

WELLINGTON PAGE 57

Windmill

PAARL PAGE 56

Area

R304

N 1

anville aaifontein

Klapmuts

R303

Bellville

R 44

R 45

Wemmershoek

Pniel

Kuilsrivier

Kylemore

STELLENBOSCH PAGES 58-59

R310

FRANSCHHOEK PAGE 54

Faure

Firgrove

Hottentots-

Holland

Nat. Res.

Somerset West

R321

N 2

Strand

Sir Lowry's Pass

False Bay

GORDON'S BAY PAGE 55

Grabouw

Elgin

Scale 1 : 160 00

Malmesbury 29km

Stellenbosch 11km
Stellenbosch 9km

18° 50'

Copyright © Map Studio MMI

| tarred | under | untarred |
| construction |

**Freeway &
National Road**

Main Road

Secondary Road

Route Markers

Distances in Kilom

Mountain Passes

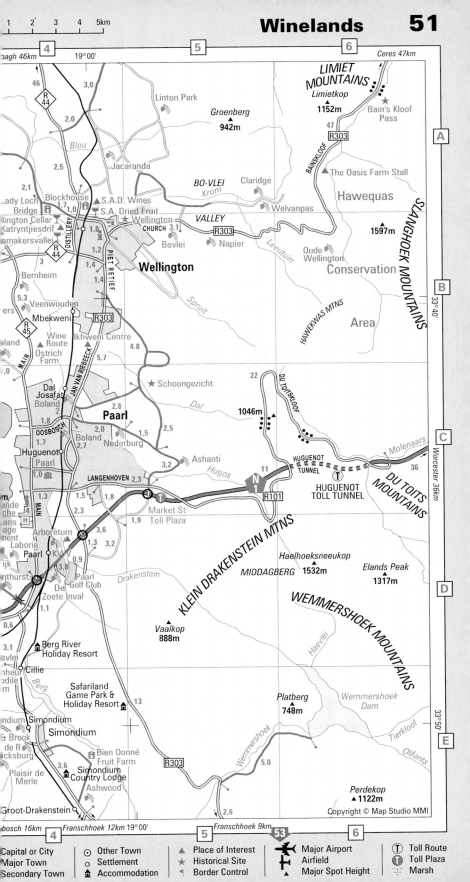

Klipheuwel 16km · 50 · 18° 50' · Paarl 24km

A

3,1
24
Klapmuts
Heen en Weer
Ostrich Farm
Anura Vineyards
Glen
Carlou
Klein Simonsvlei
Bodega
4,5
De Meye
KLAPMUTSKOP
5,8
Backsberg
Le Bonheur
Wiesenhof
Game Park
2,8
Hoopenburg
Eaglevlei
Muldersvlei
▲ 522m
4
Warwick
Laibach
1,7
Klapmuts
Lievland
SKURWEBERG

Cape Town 29km · 33°50'
29
1,4 · R101 · 5,2
Kraaifontein
5,3
Villiera
Klawervlei
De Novo
4,8 · R304
R 44
2
Slaley
3,1
Kanonkop
Uitkyk
Muratie
Kanonko
914m · ▲
Kraaifontein
BOTFONTEIN
12

Bellville 12km
3,6
Swart
BOTTELARY
4
Mulderbosch
Simonsig
2,2 · KROMME · RHEE
1,2
Koelenhof
1,5
KOELENHOF
KNORHOEK
Knorhoek
Klippies
3,3
Delheim

B
Kuilsrivier 12km
Hazendal
12
Goede Hoop
Bottelary
Bouwland
Beyerskloof
1,9 · 1,9
Hartenberg
Devon Valley
Protea
J.C. Le Roux H
2
Devon
Hill
Meinert
3,5
L'Avenir
Louisenhof
6
Wine Route
Niet Voorbij
Research Farm
3,4
Remhoogte
Morgenhof
Rustenberg
The H
Stelle
Idasvallei
Dam

Kaapzicht
Fort Simon
Louisvale
2,9
Sylvanvale
1,3
Clos Malverne
Mooiplaas
RIBBOKKOP
Middelvlei
The Bergkelder
Oude
Libertas
Du
Toit
1,7
Krom
JAN
CELLIERS
LELIE
HÉLLSHOOGTE
Hellshoogte
Pass
6,1
Rozen

C
Bellville 22km · 34°00'
Zevenwacht
L'Émigré
Jordan
Uiterwyk
KANONKOP
349m
STELLENBOSCH
KLOOF
Neethlingshof
4,5
Verdun
Overgaauw
Stellenbosch
Farmers
2,1
Vredenheim
MERRIMAN
Oom
Samie
se Winkel
D'Ouwe Werf
Stellenbosch
H
Stellenbosch
Le Riche
Aan die Oever H
STELL
1167m ▲
Saxenburg
POLKADRAAI
Goedgeloof
Carisbrooke
5,2
Vlottenburg
1,3 · 1,4
Eersterivier
Fleurbaix
Libertas
1,7
Assegaa
Nat

Jacobsdal
M 12
VLAEBERG
Reyneke
7
Boschkloof
Brandy Cellar
Van Ryn
Kleine Zalze
Stellenbosch
Golf Course
2,1
Blaauwklippen
Vriesenhof
BLAAUWKLIPPEN

D
Armani
4
Lynedoch
Drie Gewels
113m
Spier
Bonte
1,3
3,3
**STELLENBOSCH
AIRFIELD**
3,7
Blue Creek
3,6
Waterford
Stellenzicht

22
Eersterivier
R310
Welmoed
1,4
ANNANDALE
4,2
0,7
Graceland
Audacia
3,3
Rust en Vrede
Dombeya Farm

Eersterivier
Cape Town 28km · Mitchells Plain 10km
10
Dovecot
Meerlust
5,5
Somerbosch
Alto
Longridge
Grangehurst
Helderkruin
Uva Mira
De Trafford
HELDERBERG
The Dome
▲ 1137m

E
Faure
Faure
Croydon
Dellrust
Post
House
Helderberg
Papyrus
WINERY
J.P.
Bredell
Stonewall
Avontuur
Yonder Hill
2,9
Cordoba
Helderberg
Nature Reserve
Erinvale Es
& Golf Clu

Muizenberg 22km
22
Vergenoegd
28
1,2
Khayelitsha
Macassar
MACASSAR
22
N 2
5,4 · R102
5,4
0,9
Firgrove
MAIN
3,9
1,8
Groot Paardevlei
Lord Charles
3,3 H
Erinva
Verge
Morgenst

Macassar
Beach
Firgrove
4
5,7
Somerset West
Somerset West
Helderberg
LOURENSFORD
Lourens River Bridge
6,3

False Bay
Groot
Paardevlei
2,2
20

Gordon's Bay 12km · 18° 50' · Grabouw 20km · Sir Lowry's

tarred under untarred construction
Freeway & National Road
N 1 · R 33 · R523
Main Road
Secondary Road
Route Markers
15 · 22
Distances in Kilo
Mountain Passes

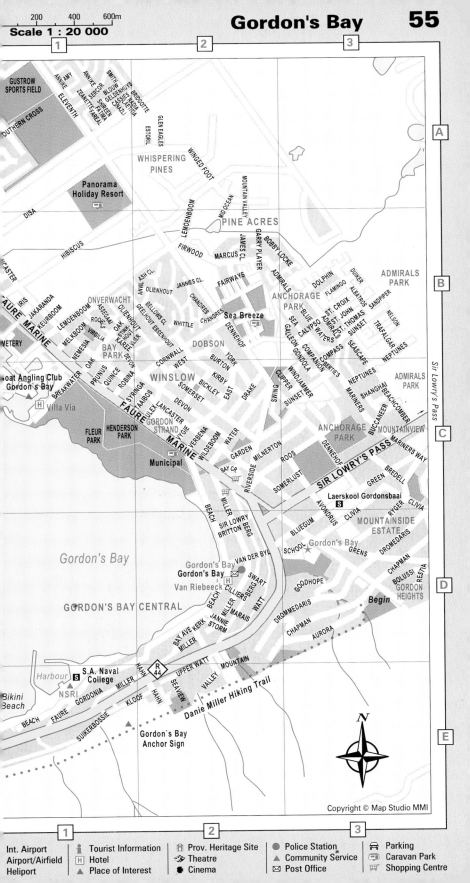

Scale 1 : 20 000

200   400   600m

1   **2**   **3**

A

GUSTROW
SPORTS FIELD

SOUTHERN CROSS

ANNIE

ANN.IKE

AMY

SMITH

SERCOR

BLOUW

GELDENHUYS

BRIGOTTE

CASSIES

NETHA

SAMZI

EILEEN

ELEVENTH

ZEANETTE

FAREIL

SINREEN

FATIMA

ESTORIL

GLEN EAGLES

WINGED FOOT

WHISPERING
PINES

Panorama
Holiday Resort

DISA

HIBISCUS

LEMOENBOOM

MOUNTAIN VALLEY

MID OCEAN

FIRWOOD

MARCUS

JAMES CL.

GARRY PLAYER

BOBBY LOCKE

PINE ACRES

B

CASTER

IRIS

JAKARANDA

KEURBOOM

MARINE

CEMETERY

FAURE

OAK

MELKBOOM

NEMESIA

LEMOENBOOM

ONVERWACHT

ASSEGAAI

ROOIKO

OLIENHOUT

GEELHOUT

OAK

STINK-HOUT

VIRGILIA

KAREEHOUT

DEVON

ANVIL

ASH CL.

OLIENHOUT

BELLOWS CL.

ESSENHOUT

WHITTLE

JANNIES CL.

CHANDRES

CHANDRES

FAIRWAYS

ADMIRALS

SEA

DOLPHIN

FLAMINGO

DUIKER

ALBATROS

SANDPIPER

ST. CROIX

ST. JOHN

ST. THOMAS

NELSON

TRAFALGAR

NEPTUNES

**ADMIRALS
PARK**

Sea Breeze

DENNEHOF

ANCHORAGE
PARK

BLUE WATERS

CALYPSO

ADMIRALS

SEERTIES

COMPASS

SUNSET

SEASCAPE

BAY
PARK

PRUNUS

OAK

QUINCE

ROBINA

SYRINGA

TAAIBOS

CORNWALL

WEST

DOBSON

YORK

BURTON

KIRBY

GALLEON

GONDOLA

COMPANION

NEPTUNES

**ADMIRALS
PARK**

SHANGHAI

BEACHCOMBER

Boat Angling Club
Gordon's Bay

BREAKWATER

Villa Via

WINSLOW

SOMERSET

BICKLEY

EAST

DRAKE

CLIPPER

SWING

SUNSET

WINDJAMMER

MARINERS

BUCCANEER

MOUNTAINVIEW

C

FLEUR
PARK

HENDERSON
PARK

FAURE

MARINE

GORDON
STRAND

LANCASTER

LYGIE

VERBENA

WILDEBOOM

WATER

GARDEN

MILNERTON

ROOS

SOMERLUST

**ANCHORAGE
PARK**

DENNEHOF

SIR LOWRY'S PASS

GREEN

BREDELL

MARINERS WAY

Municipal

BAY CR.

RIVERSIDE

Laerskool Gordonsbaai

AVONDRUS

CLIVIA

RYGER

CLIVIA

BEACH

MILLER

SIR LOWRY

BERG

BRITTON

BLUEGUM

GRENS

DROMEDARIS

**MOUNTAINSIDE
ESTATE**

SCHOOL

Gordon's Bay

CHAPMAN

BOLUSSI

RESTA

**GORDON
HEIGHTS**

VAN DER BYL

Gordon's Bay

Gordon's Bay
Van Riebeeck

SWART

CILLIERSBERG

GODHOPE

D

GORDON'S BAY CENTRAL

BAY

AVE

KERK

MILLER

BEACH

JANNIE

STORM

MARAIS

WATT

DROMMEDARIS

CHAPMAN

AURORA

Begin

Harbour

S.A. Naval
College

NSRI

GORDONIA

MILLER

HAHN

UPPER WATT

SEAVIEW

MOUNTAIN

VALLEY

Danie Miller Hiking Trail

R
44

Bikini
Beach

BEACH

FAURE

SUIKERBOSSIE

KLOOF

HAHN

Gordon's Bay
Anchor Sign

N

Copyright © Map Studio MMI

E

Sir Lowry's Pass

1   **2**   **3**

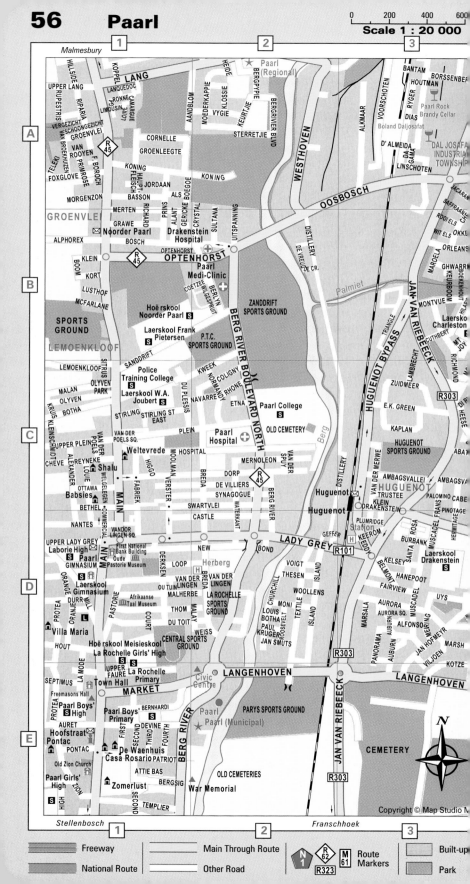

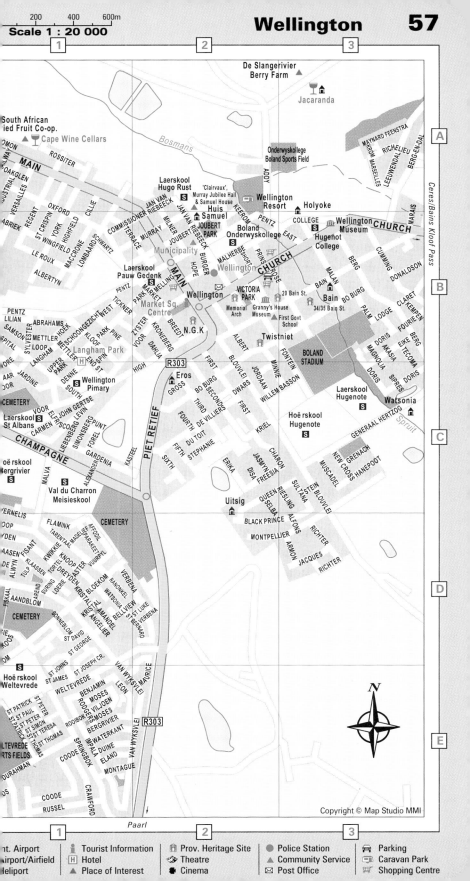

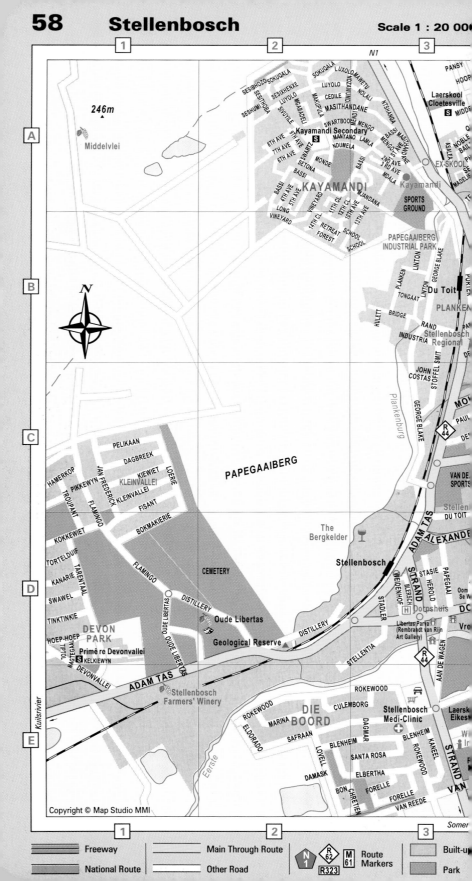

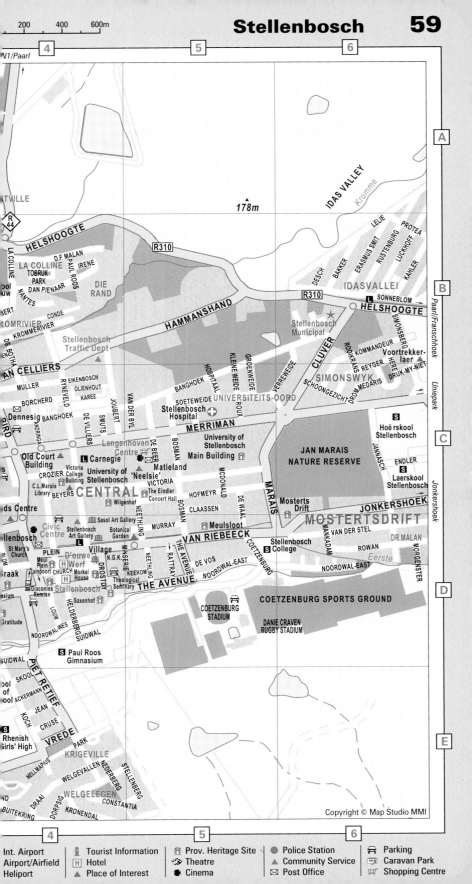

An area of magnificent views, panoramic landscapes and towering cliffs, crystal-clear streams, an abundance of trees and indigenous flora, the Breede River Valley is the largest of the Western Cape's three fruit and wine producing valleys. Mountains, the highest peaks of

which are capped with snow in winter, surround this heavily cultivated region, graced with orchards, vineyards and wheatlands.

The Breede River Valley is also known as the Wine Belt of the Western Cape, with a harmoniously balanced terrain and climate. Innovation

THE BREEDE RIVER GIVES THE REGION ITS NAME

and pride are the main ingredients of the region's winemakers, resulting in their success and prominence.

Ceres, a principal town in the area, was named after the Roman goddess of fertility, which should come as no surprise. It is surely one of the most fertile farming areas in South Africa. With the Piketberg and Bokkeveld areas, the region dominates South Africa's export of peaches and pears. Robertson, Worcester, McGregor and Montagu are rich in the ingredients a vintner needs to create noble wines. Cool summer breezes blow off the sea, chill winters provide rest for the vines and a fertile, lime-rich soil nourishes the future pleasures of people around the world.

Nature-lovers and those seeking tranquillity, sparkling air and fruit-off-the-tree need look no further than this lovely valley. Fifteen easily accessible towns nestle in the valley and a multitude of attractions offers the opportunity for discovery. From visits to wineries and tours of culture-rich towns to game reserve excursions, glimpses of tribal art and museums, or the outdoor excitement of mountain-biking or hiking trails, the Breede River Valley has it all! The R62 between Cape Town and Port Elizabeth winds through this area. This alternative route to Port Elizabeth passes all the main gems of the Breede River Valley.

The Cape
South Africa
Western Cape Tourism Board
www.capetourism.org

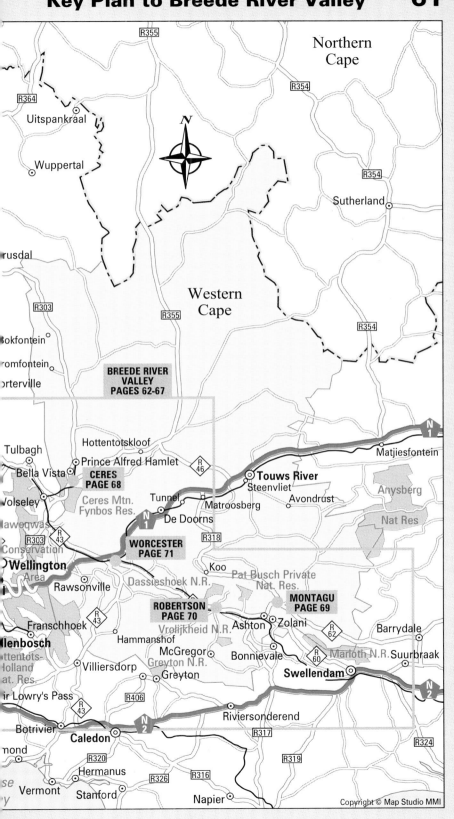

Northern
Cape

R354

R355

R364

Uitspankraal

Sutherland

R354

N

Wuppertal

rusdal

Western
Cape

R303

R355

okfontein

R354

omfontein

orterville

**BREEDE RIVER
VALLEY
PAGES 62-67**

Hottentotskloof

Tulbagh

Prince Alfred Hamlet

Matjiesfontein

N1

Bella Vista

**CERES
PAGE 68**

R46

Touws River

olseley

Ceres Mtn.
Fynbos Res.

Tunnel

Steenvliet

Anysberg

aweqwas

N1

Matroosberg

Avondrust

Nat Res

R303

R43

De Doorns

Conservation

R318

**Wellington
Area**

**WORCESTER
PAGE 71**

Koo

Pat Busch Private
Nat. Res.

Rawsonville

Dassieshoek N.R.

**MONTAGU
PAGE 69**

Franschhoek

R43

**ROBERTSON
PAGE 70**

Vrolijkheid N.R.

Ashton

Zolani

R62

Barrydale

llenbosch

Hammanshof

McGregor

Bonnievale

R60

Marloth N.R. Suurbraak

ttentots-
Iolland
at. Res.

Villiersdorp

Greyton N.R.

Greyton

Swellendam

N2

ir Lowry's Pass

R43

R406

N2

Riviersonderend

Botrivier

R317

N2

R324

mond

Caledon

R320

R319

se

Hermanus

R326

R316

ry

Vermont

Stanford

Napier

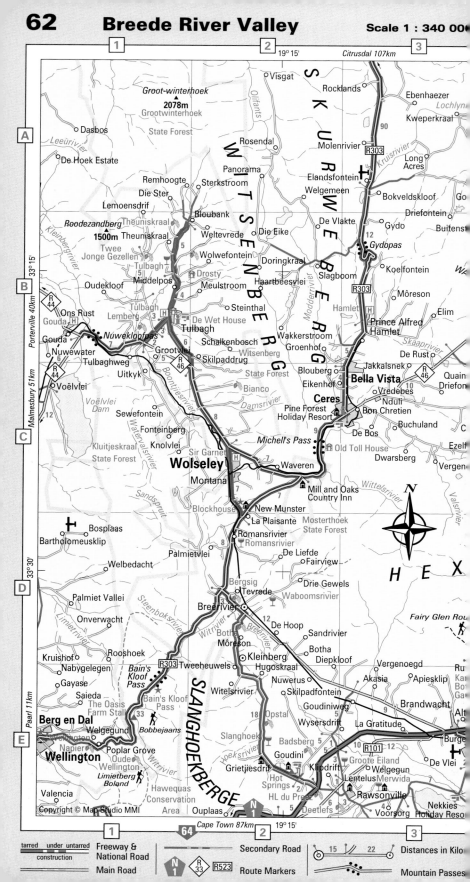

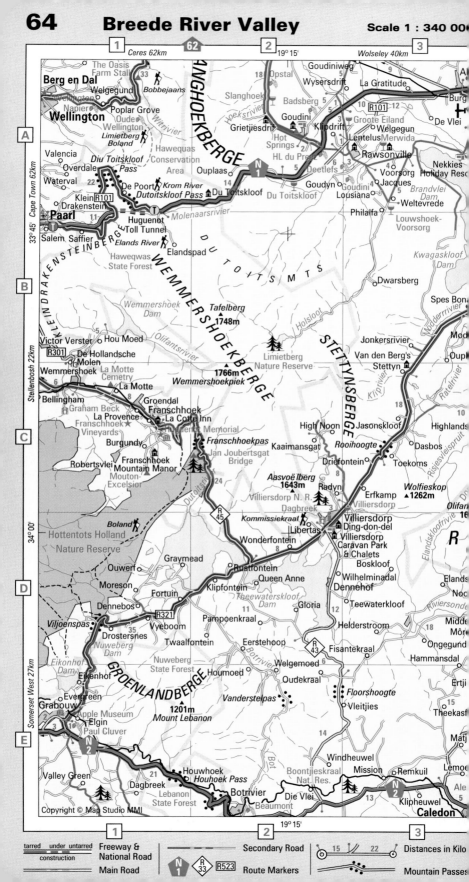

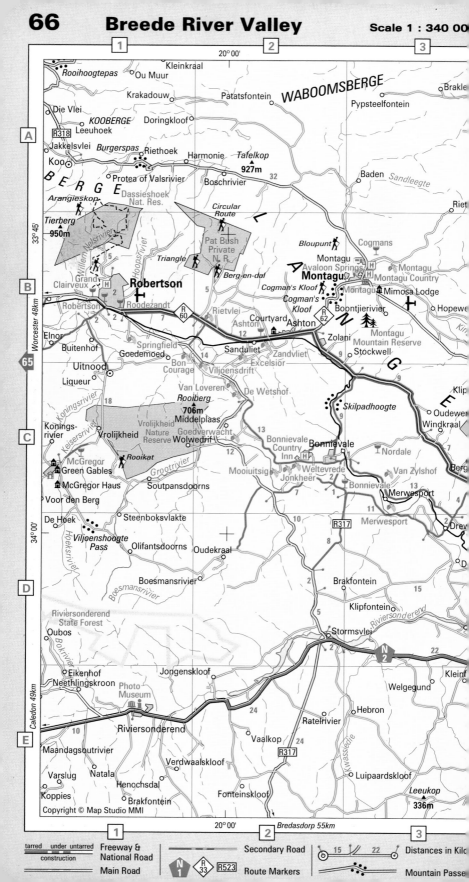

The West Coast is a region of extreme beauty and contrast. Stretching over 400km from south to north, the region and its people offer visitors plenty of sunshine and a surprising variety of travel destinations. To the west, the region borders the Atlantic Ocean. The solitary coast's scenic beauty is challenged only by rich culinary experiences of plump mussels, oysters, calamari, crayfish and abalone in season or linefish pulled from the Benguela Current's cold waters and fried to gold. All are best enjoyed at a sunset fishbraai enlivened by a good wine and the spontaneous, light-hearted banter of hard-working, hard-playing locals.

The area is a bird-watcher's paradise – cawing, white-breasted gulls wheel high on the seawind above thousands of gannets with their distinct, yellow-painted faces, while flamingoes colour the sky pink and swift, darting terns give the lie to the martial imperiousness of ever-aloof penguins. In addition, every year migrating whales visit the coastal waters from July. The eastern border is formed by a belt of mountains with fascinating, often awe-inspiring rock formations. The Cederberg Wilderness area offers visitors a face-to-face encounter with nature at its most unspoiled as well as rock paintings that dramatically pre-date the world as we know it. Adjacent to the mountains is the Swartland, well known for its undulating wheat fields, vineyards, wineries and outdoor activities.

SPRING FLOWERS AT "RAMSKOP" NATURE RESERVE

Further north, visitors encounter the fertile Olifant's River Valley and the vast plains of the Knersvlakte with its wealth of indigenous succulent plants. The Olifant's River Valley is cultivated intensively with an emphasis on citrus and other fruits, vegetables and vine-yards. The West Coast and its hinterland is a cultural experience of museums, monuments and mission stations such as Mamre and Wupperthal. It offers activities such as exploration in a fossil park, hang-gliding, sky-diving, mountain-biking, 4 x 4 routes, watersports and hiking. The experience extends also to a superb array of local wines, fresh seafood and other delectable fare, as well as a health-giving herbal drink, rooibos tea. In spring, carpets of wild flowers cover the region from the coast to the mountains. Spring flowers and fynbos are a constantly changing wonder attracting hikers and nature-lovers throughout the year.

TheCape
South Africa

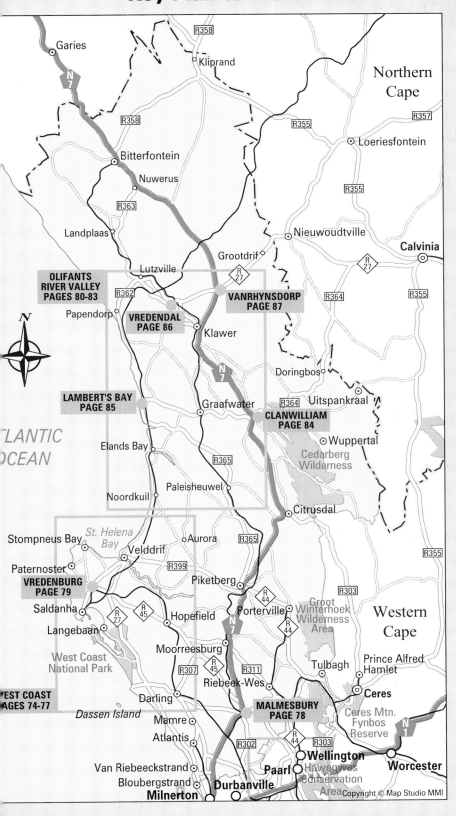

Garies

R358

Kliprand

N7

Northern Cape

R357

R358

Loeriesfontein

Bitterfontein

Nuwerus

R355

R363

Nieuwoudtville

Landplaas

Calvinia

Lutzville

Grootdrif

R27

OLIFANTS RIVER VALLEY PAGES 80-83

R362

VANRHYNSDORP PAGE 87

R27

VREDENDAL PAGE 86

Papendorp

Klawer

R364

R355

N7

Doringbos

LAMBERT'S BAY PAGE 85

Graafwater

R364

Uitspankraal

CLANWILLIAM PAGE 84

Elands Bay

Wuppertal

Cedarberg Wilderness

R365

Noordkuil

Paleisheuwel

Citrusdal

St. Helena Bay

Aurora

R365

R355

Stompneus Bay

Velddrif

ATLANTIC OCEAN

R399

Piketberg

R303

Paternoster

VREDENBURG PAGE 79

R44

Groot Winterhoek Wilderness Area

Western Cape

Saldanha

R27

R45

Hopefield

Porterville

R44

Langebaan

Moorreesburg

Prince Alfred Hamlet

West Coast National Park

R307

R45

R311

Tulbagh

Ceres

Riebeek-Wes

WEST COAST PAGES 74-77

Dassen Island

Darling

MALMESBURY PAGE 78

Ceres Mtn. Fynbos Reserve

Mamre

N

Atlantis

R302

R44

R303

Worcester

Van Riebeeckstrand

Wellington

Hawequas Conservation Area

Bloubergstrand

Paarl

Durbanville

Milnerton

Copyright © Map Studio MMI

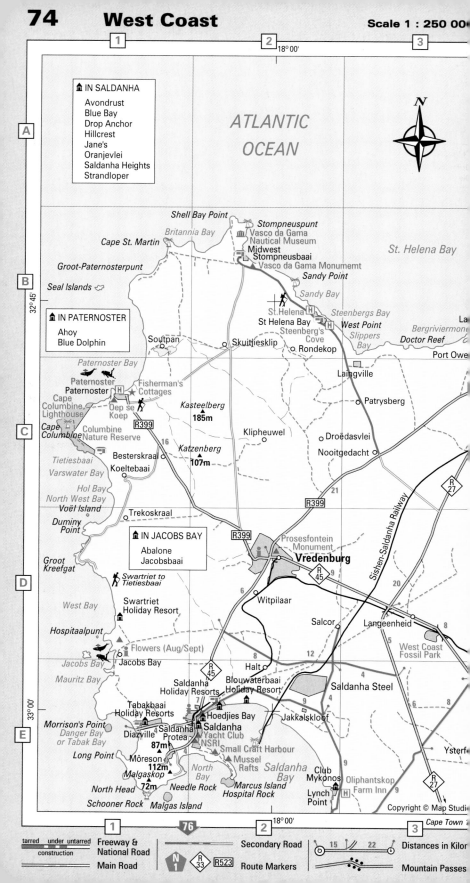

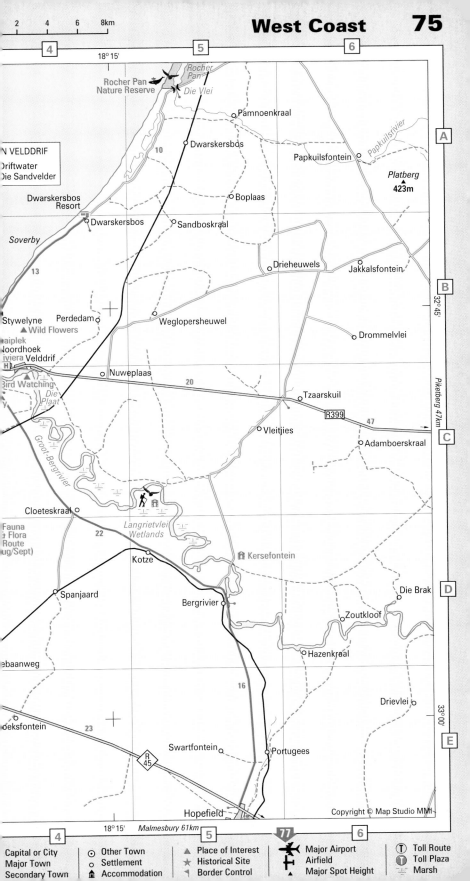

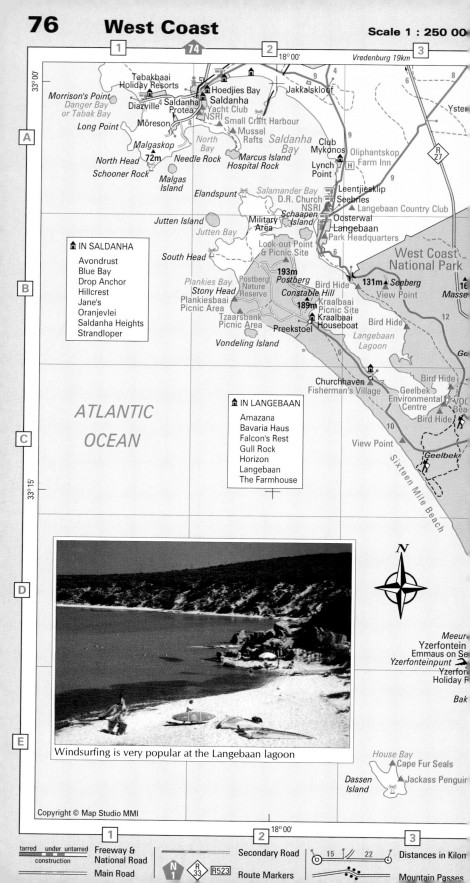

IN SALDANHA

Avondrust
Blue Bay
Drop Anchor
Hillcrest
Jane's
Oranjevlei
Saldanha Heights
Strandloper

IN LANGEBAAN

Amazana
Bavaria Haus
Falcon's Rest
Gull Rock
Horizon
Langebaan
The Farmhouse

ATLANTIC
OCEAN

Windsurfing is very popular at the Langebaan lagoon

Copyright © Map Studio MMI

tarred	under	untarred	**Freeway &**					**Secondary Road**				**Distances in Kilom**
construction			**National Road**									
			Main Road					**Route Markers**				**Mountain Passes**

Vredenburg 19km

West Coast
National Park

Langebaan
Lagoon

Sixteen Mile Beach

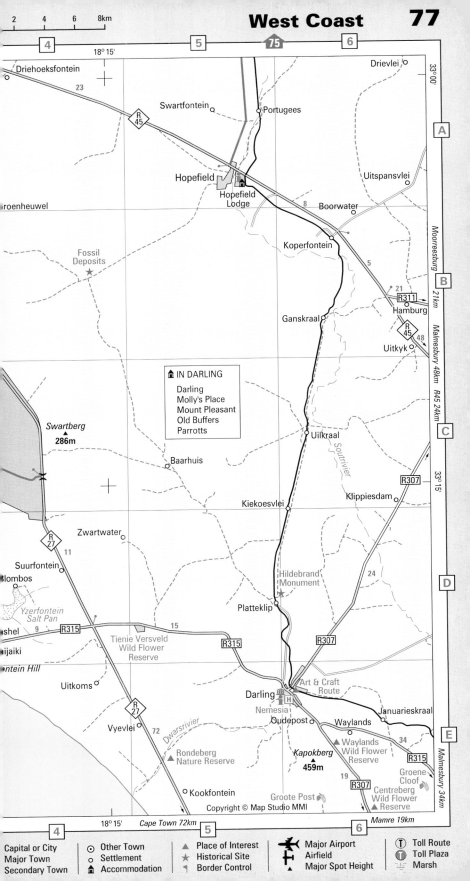

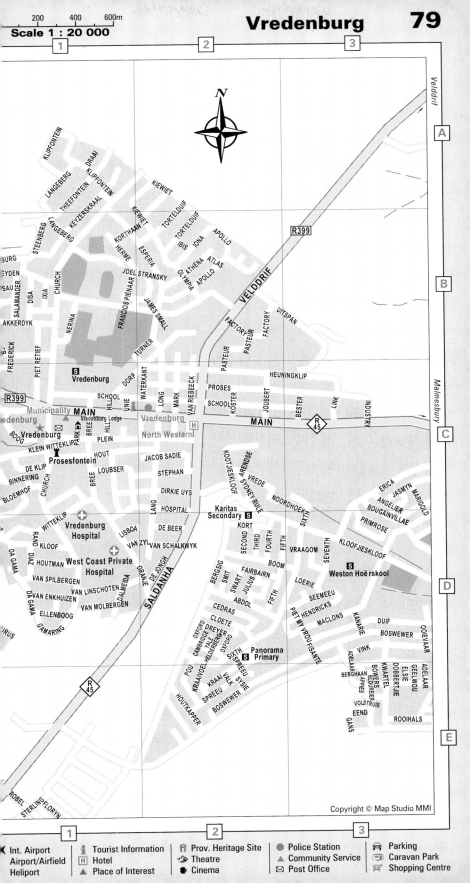

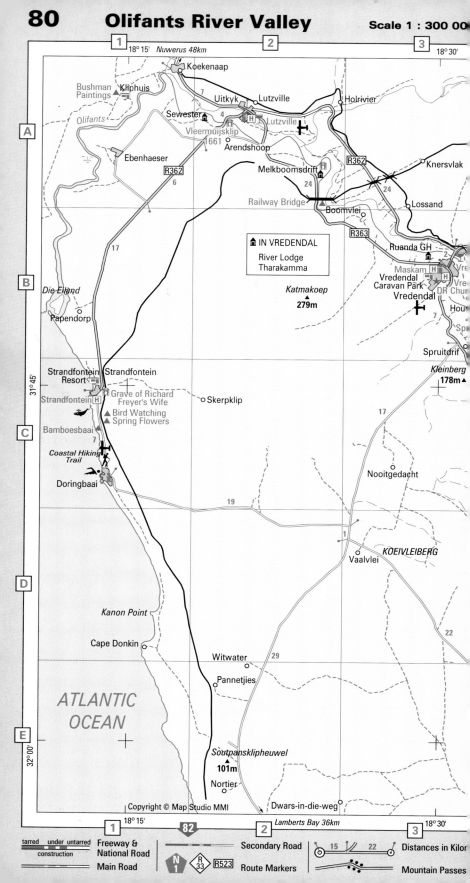

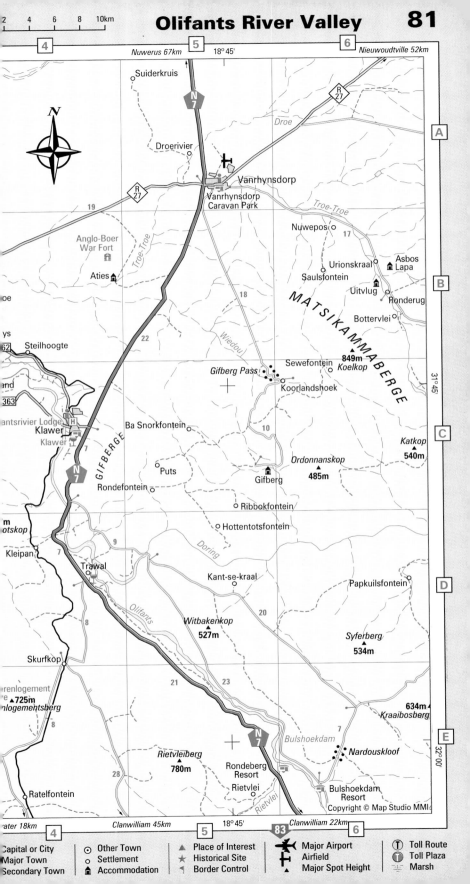

2 4 6 8 10km

N

Suiderkruis

N 7

R 27

Droerivier

Droe

A

Vanrhynsdorp

R 27

Vanrhynsdorp
Caravan Park

19

Troe-Troe

Nuwepos

17

Urionskraal

Asbos
Lapa

Saulsfontein

Anglo-Boer
War Fort

Uitvlug

Aties

Ronderug

18

Bottervlei

B

Troe-Troe

M A T S I K A M M A B E R G E

22

Wiedou

Sewefontein

849m

Koelkop

31° 45'

Gifberg Pass

Koorlandshoek

Steilhoogte

462

363

Ba Snorkfontein

10

Katkop
540m

C

ntsrivier Lodge

Klawer

Klawer

N 7

G I F B E R G E

Puts

Gifberg

Ordonnanskop
485m

Rondefontein

Ribbokfontein

Hottentotsfontein

otskop

Doring

9

Kleipan

Papkuilsfontein

D

Trawal

Kant-se-kraal

20

Olifants

8

Witbakenkop
527m

Syferberg
534m

Skurfkop

renlogement
re
nlogementsberg

▲725m

21

23

634m
Kraaibosberg

7

8

N 7

Bulshoekdam

E

Nardouskloof

32° 00'

Rietvleiberg
780m

Rondeberg
Resort

Bulshoekdam
Resort

28

Rietvlei

Rietvlei

Ratelfontein

Copyright © Map Studio MMI

rater 18km

Capital or City   ⊙ Other Town   ▲ Place of Interest   Major Airport   ⊤ Toll Route

Major Town   ○ Settlement   ★ Historical Site   Airfield   ⊤ Toll Plaza

Secondary Town   ⌂ Accommodation   ◄ Border Control   Major Spot Height   Marsh

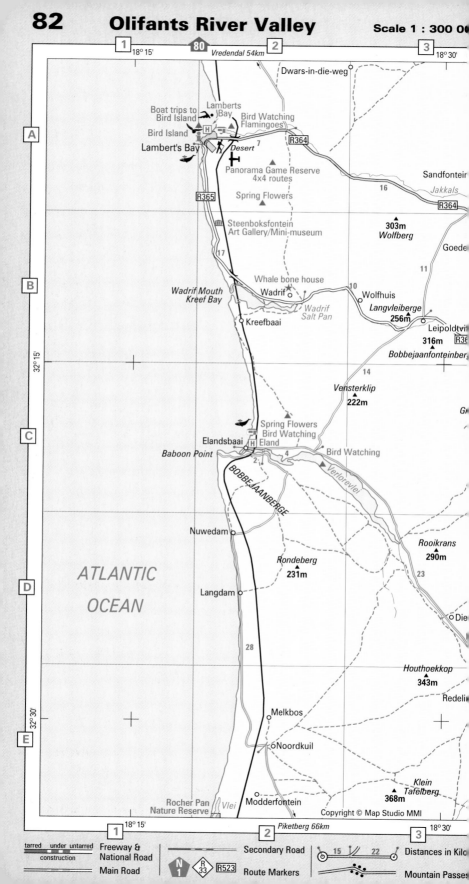

ATLANTIC
OCEAN

Places and features:

- Dwars-in-die-weg
- Boat trips to Bird Island
- Lamberts Bay
- Bird Watching
- Flamingoes
- Bird Island
- Lambert's Bay
- Desert
- R364
- 7
- Sandfonteir
- Panorama Game Reserve 4x4 routes
- 16
- Jakkals
- Spring Flowers
- R365
- 303m Wolfberg
- Steenboksfontein Art Gallery/Mini-museum
- Goede
- 17
- 11
- Whale bone house
- Wadrif Mouth Kreef Bay
- Wadrif
- 10
- Wolfhuis
- Langvleiberge 256m
- Leipoldtvi
- R36
- Kreefbaai
- Wadrif Salt Pan
- 316m
- Bobbejaanfonteinber
- 14
- Vensterklip 222m
- Gr
- Spring Flowers Bird Watching Eland
- Elandsbaai
- Baboon Point
- 2
- 4
- Bird Watching
- Verlorevlei
- BOBBEJAANBERGE
- Nuwedam
- Rooikrans 290m
- Rondeberg 231m
- 23
- Langdam
- Die
- 28
- Houthoekkop 343m
- Redeli
- Melkbos
- Noordkuil
- Klein Tafelberg 368m
- Rocher Pan Nature Reserve
- Vlei
- Modderfontein

Coordinates: 18° 15', 18° 30', 32° 15', 32° 30'

Vredendal 54km

Piketberg 66km

Legend:

tarred   under   untarred   construction   Freeway & National Road   Main Road

N1   R33   R523   Secondary Road   Route Markers

15   22   Distances in Kilo   Mountain Passes

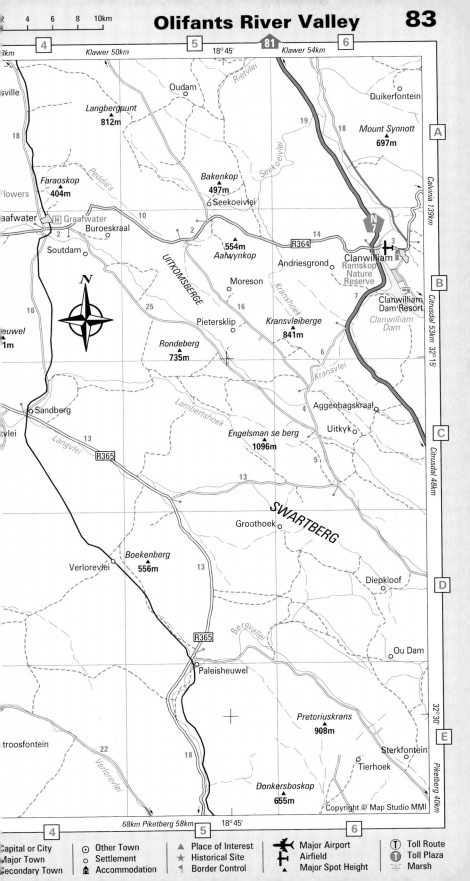

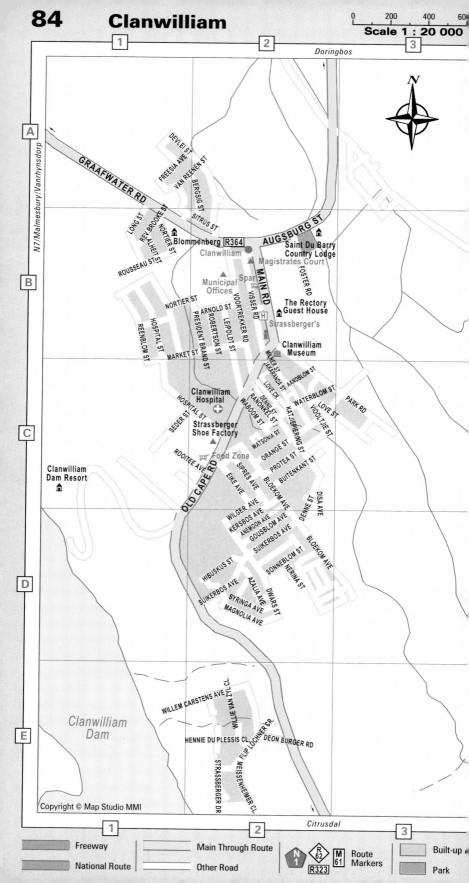

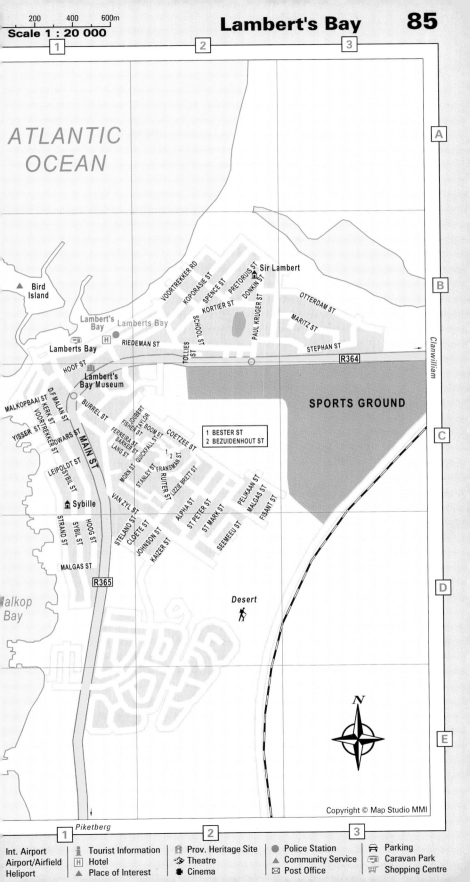

Scale 1 : 20 000

200 400 600m

ATLANTIC
OCEAN

Bird
Island

Lambert's
Bay

Lamberts Bay

Lamberts Bay

VOORTREKKER RD

KOPORASIE ST

SPENCE ST

KORTIER ST

SCHOOLS ST

PRETORIUS ST

DONKIN ST

Sir Lambert

PAUL KRUGER ST

OTTERDAM ST

MARITZ ST

RIEDEMAN ST

TOLLIES ST

STEPHAN ST

HOOF ST

Lambert's
Bay Museum

R364

Clanwilliam

MALKOPBAAI ST

D.F MALAN ST

KERK ST

VOORTREKKER ST

EDWARDS ST

YISSER ST

BURREL ST

MAIN ST

LEIPOLDT ST

SYBIL ST

Sybille

STRAND ST

SYBIL ST

HOOG ST

MALGAS ST

R365

alkop
Bay

JOUBERT ST

FISHER ST

TAYLOR

FERREIRA ST

BARKER ST

LANG ST

MORN ST

QUICKFALL ST

BOOM ST

COETZEE ST

STANLEY ST

FRANSMAN ST

RUITER ST

LIZZIE BRETT ST

VAN ZYL ST

ALPHA ST

ST PETER ST

ST MARK ST

PELIKAAN ST

MALGAS ST

FISANT ST

STELAND ST

CLOETE ST

JOHNSON ST

KAIZER ST

SEEMEEU ST

1 2

1 BESTER ST
2 BEZUIDENHOUT ST

SPORTS GROUND

Desert

N

Copyright © Map Studio MMI

Int. Airport
Airport/Airfield
Heliport

Tourist Information
Hotel
Place of Interest

Prov. Heritage Site
Theatre
Cinema

Police Station
Community Service
Post Office

Parking
Caravan Park
Shopping Centre

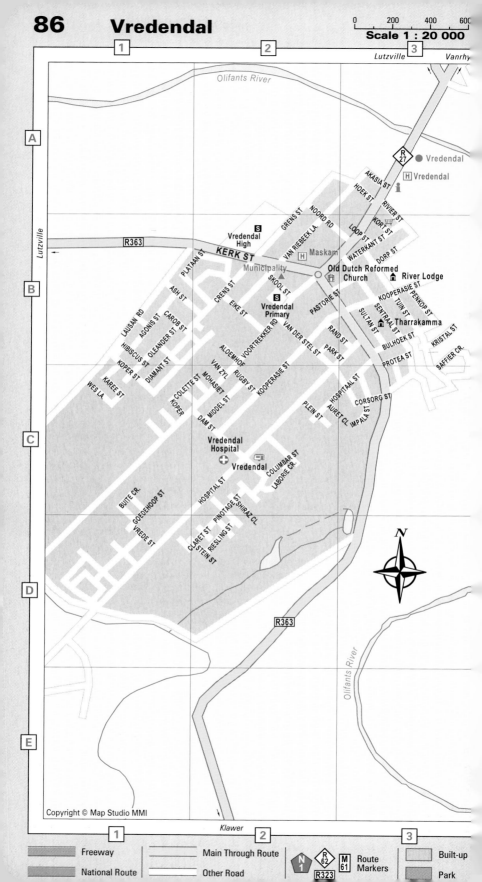

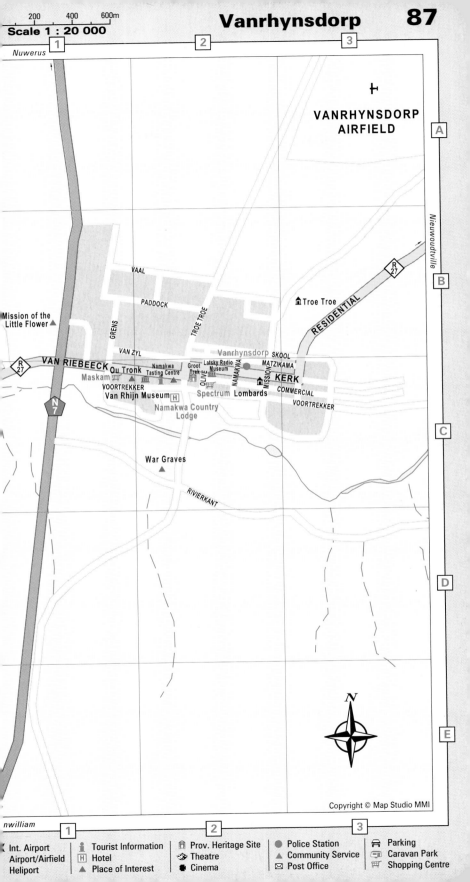

Scale 1 : 20 000

200   400   600m

Nuwerus

1   **2**   **3**

✛

VANRHYNSDORP AIRFIELD

Nieuwoudtville

A

🏛 Troe Troe

R 27

B

RESIDENTIAL

VAAL

PADDOCK

TROE TROE

GRENS

VAN ZYL

Mission of the Little Flower ▲

Vanrhynsdorp SKOOL

MATZIKAMA

R 27

VAN RIEBEECK

Ou Tronk

Namakwa Tasting Centre

Groot Trek

OLIVE

Latsky Radio Museum

NAMAKWA

MISSION

KERK

COMMERCIAL

Maskam

VOORTREKKER

Van Rhijn Museum H

Spectrum Lombards

VOORTREKKER

N 7

Namakwa Country Lodge

War Graves ▲

C

RIVIERKANT

D

E

N

Copyright © Map Studio MMI

nwilliam

1   **2**   **3**

In the most southerly region of Africa, only one hour east of Cape Town, lies the Fairest Cape's best kept secret, a fertile area surrounded by mountains and sea. Simply called the Overberg, it is the traveller's reward for breaching the mountain barriers which divide it from the rest of the country. To early settlers it represented the land beyond the mountains of Africa, a region rich in resources as well as boundless treasures.

The Overberg coast, also called the Whale Coast, has the distinction of splitting the oceans. At Cape Agulhas, the southernmost tip of the continent, the waters are cleaved into the Indian and Atlantic Oceans. The foothills of the mountains, covered in a wealth of indigenous fynbos, roll down through green and gold wheat and sheep country to the lighthouse here. Apart from the cry of seagulls and the endless beat of the surf along a holiday-friendly shoreline – which also gives rest to the wreckage of scores of luckless ships – silence prevails and solitude is easy to find.

A scattering of tiny seaside resorts in the vicinity attract regular caravaners, campers and fishermen. In contrast is Hermanus, a bustling town where crowds flock to watch migrating whales between June and November. The region offers visitors a myriad other activities, such as golf, hiking, birdwatching, canoeing, mountain biking, architectural tours, historical tours, fynbos and flower trails and, of course, unending opportunities to indulge in fine food and wine.

WAENHUISKRANS IN THE ARNISTON AREA

This superb coastal area, stretching from Hangklip to the mouth of the Breede River, can be approached from the Cape Peninsula over the dramatic Sir Lowry's Pass along the N2 national road, or by a coastal road carved from the sea cliffs from Gordon's Bay, through the Kogelberg Biosphere – the only one in South Africa. The area can also be journeyed into from other regions of the Western Cape Province such as the Winelands, the Garden Route, the Breede River and the Klein Karoo.

TheCape
South Africa

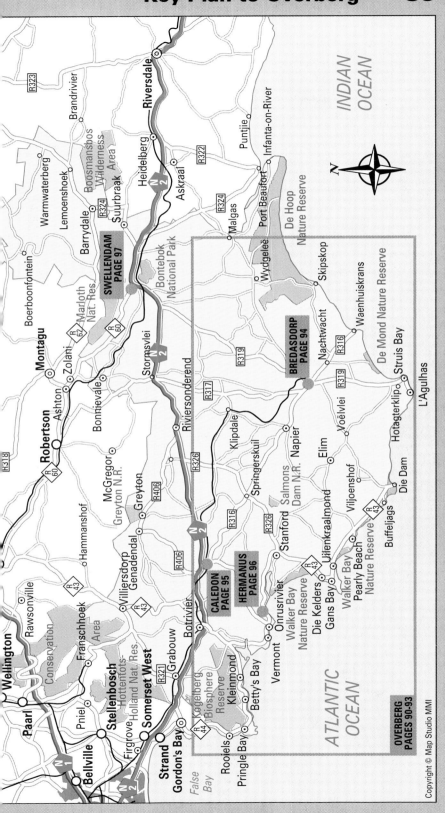

INDIAN OCEAN

ATLANTIC OCEAN

False Bay

R323

Brandrivier

Riversdale

Warmwaterberg

Lemoenshoek

Boosmansbos Wilderness Area

Heidelberg

Suurbraak

Askraal

Puntjie

Infanta-on-River

Port Beaufort

Barrydale

R324

R322

Malgas

De Hoop Nature Reserve

Boerboonfontein

Montagu

Zolani

R62

R60

Ashton

SWELLENDAM PAGE 97

Marloth Nat. Res.

Bontebok National Park

Stormsvlei

Wydgeleë

Skipskop

Waenhuiskrans

Robertson

R318

R60

Bontievale

R324

R319

BREDASDORP PAGE 94

Nachtwacht

R316

De Mond Nature Reserve

Struis Bay

Hammanshof

McGregor Greyton N.R.

Greyton

Riviersonderend

R317

Klipdale

Napier

R319

Voëlvlei

Hotagterklip

L'Agulhas

Rawsonville

Villiersdorp

Genadendal

R406

R326

Springerskuil

Salmons Dam N.R.

Elim

Viljoenshof

Die Dam

Franschhoek Conservation Area

R43

R316

R326

Stanford

Uilenkraalmond

R43

Buffeljags

Wellington

Paarl

Hottentots-Holland Nat. Res.

Grabouw

Botrivier

CALEDON PAGE 95

HERMANUS PAGE 96

Onrusrivier

Walker Bay Nature Reserve

Die Kelders

Gans Bay

Walker Bay

Pearly Beach Nature Reserve

R43

Pniel

Stellenbosch

R321

Vermont

Betty's Bay

Kleinmond

Kogelberg Biosphere Reserve

R44

Bellville

Firgrove

Somerset West

Strand

Gordon's Bay

Rooiels

Pringle Bay

OVERBERG PAGES 90-93

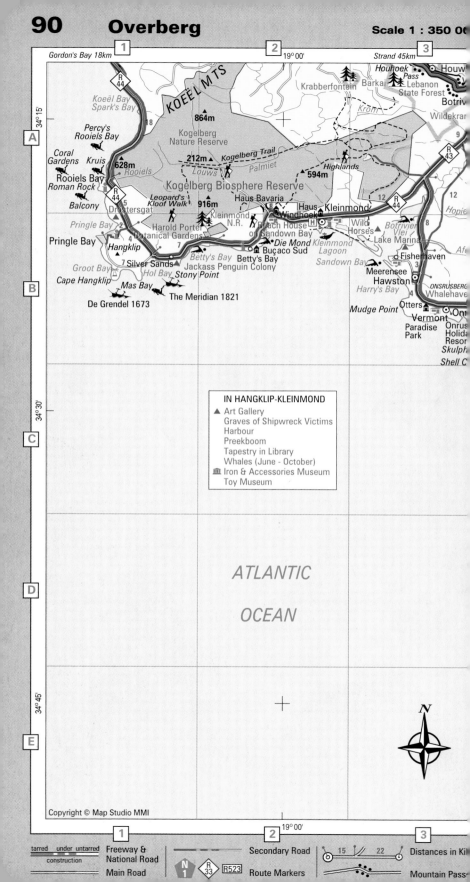

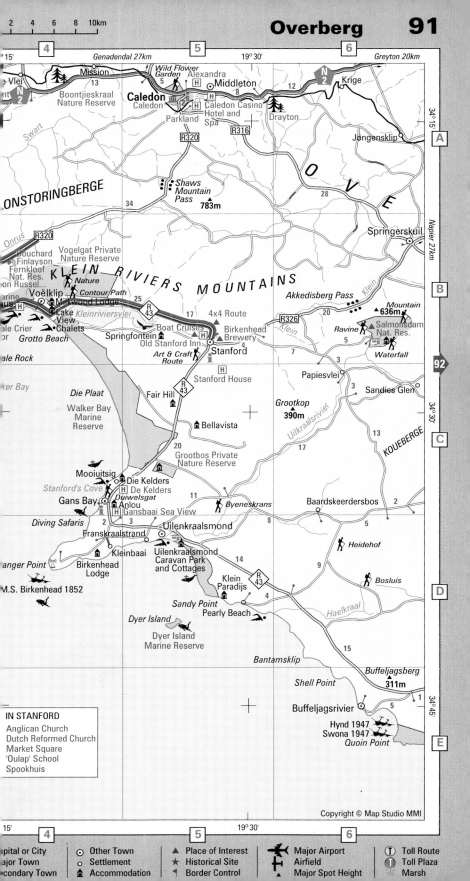

2   4   6   8   10km

15'

Mission   13

Wild Flower Garden

Alexandra

Middleton

34° 15'

Boontjieskraal Nature Reserve

Caledon
Caledon

Parkland

Caledon Casino Hotel and Spa

Drayton

Krige

A

Swart

R320

R316

Jongensklip

O V E

Shaws Mountain Pass
783m

28

34

ONSTORINGBERGE

Springerskuil

Napier 27km

R320

Onrus

Bouchard Finlayson
Fernkloof Nat. Res.

Vogelgat Private Nature Reserve

KLEIN RIVIERS MOUNTAINS

Akkedisberg Pass

B

on Russel

Voëlklip

Nature Contour Path

Milkwood Lodge

25

R43

17

4x4 Route

Klein

R326

20

Mountain
636m

Salmonsdam Nat. Res.

ale Crier

Lake View Chalets

Kleinriviersvlei

Boat Cruises

Springfontein

Old Stanford Inn

Birkenhead Brewery

Ravine

Waterfall

5

Grotto Beach

Art & Craft Route

Stanford

4

7

3

92

ale Rock

Die Plaat

R43

Stanford House

Papiesvlei

3

34° 30'

ker Bay

Walker Bay Marine Reserve

Fair Hill

Bellavista

Grootkop
390m

Uilkraalsrivier

Sandies Glen

13

C

17

KOUEBERGE

20

Grootbos Private Nature Reserve

Mooiuitsig

Die Kelders

Stanford's Cove

De Kelders

Gans Bay

Duiwelsgat

Anlou

11

Byeneskrans

Baardskeerdersbos

2

Diving Safaris

Gansbaai Sea View

8

5

Heidehof

D

Franskraalstrand

3

Uilenkraalsmond

anger Point

Kleinbaai

Birkenhead Lodge

Uilenkraalsmond Caravan Park and Cottages

14

9

Bosluis

M.S. Birkenhead 1852

Klein Paradijs

R43

4

Haelkraal

Sandy Point

Pearly Beach

Dyer Island

15

Dyer Island Marine Reserve

Bantamsklip

Buffeljagsberg

34° 45'

Shell Point

311m

1

Buffeljagsrivier

5

Hynd 1947
Swona 1947
Quoin Point

E

IN STANFORD
Anglican Church
Dutch Reformed Church
Market Square
'Oulap' School
Spookhuis

15'

pital or City	⊙ Other Town	▲ Place of Interest	✖ Major Airport	Ⓣ Toll Route
ajor Town	○ Settlement	★ Historical Site	✈ Airfield	Ⓣ Toll Plaza
condary Town	▣ Accommodation	◀ Border Control	▲ Major Spot Height	Marsh

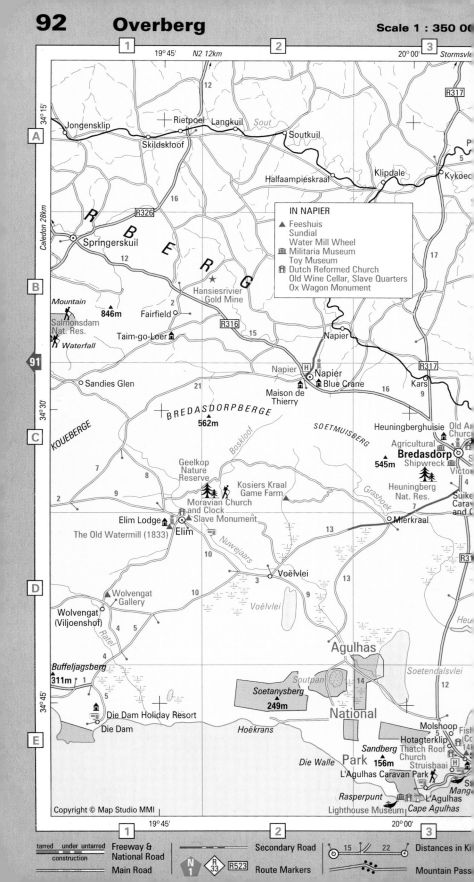

19° 45'   N2 12km   20° 00'   Stormsvle

R317

A
Jongensklip
Rietpoel   Langkuil   Sout
Skildskloof   Soutkuil
12
Halfaampieskraal   Klipdale   Kykoec
5
P

34° 15'
Caledon 28km

16
R326
Springerskuil
12
★ Hansiesrivier
Gold Mine

IN NAPIER
▲ Feeshuis
  Sundial
  Water Mill Wheel
🏛 Militaria Museum
  Toy Museum
⛪ Dutch Reformed Church
  Old Wine Cellar, Slave Quarters
  Ox Wagon Monument

17

B
Mountain
846m   Fairfield ○   2
Salmonsdam
Nat. Res.
Waterfall   Taim-go-Loer 🏛   R316   15   Napier

91
○ Sandies Glen   21   Napier 🅷 🏛 Napier
                        Blue Crane   Kars
Maison de   16   R317
Thierry   9

BREDASDORPBERGE   SOETMUISBERG   Heuningberghuisie   Old A
562m   Chur
KOUEBERGE   Boskloof   Agricultural 🏛
                        Bredasdorp ○
7   545m   Shipwreck   Victo
8   Geelkop   Grashoek   Heuningberg   Suike
    Nature   Nat. Res.   Cara
9   Reserve   Kosiers Kraal   7   and C
2   Game Farm
    Moravian Church   Mierkraal
Elim Lodge 🏛 and Clock   13
The Old Watermill (1833)   Slave Monument
                        Elim
10   Nuwejaars   3   Voëlvlei   13

D
Wolvengat   10   9
Gallery   Voëlvlei
Wolvengat
(Viljoenshof)   4   5   Heu
4
Ratel   Agulhas   Soetendalsvlei
Buffeljagsberg   Soutpan   14   12
311m   1
5   Soetanysberg
249m   National
🏛 Die Dam Holiday Resort   Molshoop   Fis
Die Dam   Hoëkrans   Hotagterklip   Co
                        Thatch Roof   14
Sandberg   Church   🅷
Die Walle   Park   156m   Struisbaai   S
L'Agulhas Caravan Park   Mang
Rasperpunt 🏛 L'Agulhas
Lighthouse Museum   Cape Agulhas

34° 30'

34° 45'

E

19° 45'   20° 00'

tarred   under   untarred
        construction

Freeway &
National Road

Main Road

Ⓝ1 ⬡ Ⓡ33 R523

Secondary Road

Route Markers

◉ 15 ⫽ 22 ◉

Distances in Kil

Mountain Pass

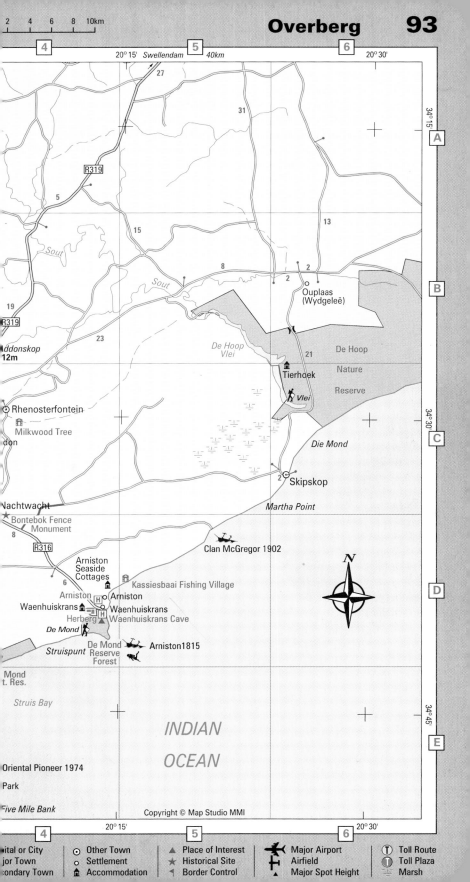

2 4 6 8 10km

4

20° 15' *Swellendam* 40km

27

31

R319

5

15

13

8 2

Sout 2

Ouplaas
(Wydgeleë)

Sout

19

R319

23

21 De Hoop

*De Hoop
Vlei*

ddonskop
12m

Tierhoek

Nature

Reserve

Vlei

Rhenosterfontein

Milkwood Tree
don

Die Mond

2 Skipskop

Nachtwacht

Martha Point

Bontebok Fence
Monument

8

R316

Clan McGregor 1902

Arniston
Seaside
Cottages

Kassiesbaai Fishing Village

6

Arniston Arniston

Waenhuiskrans Waenhuiskrans
Herberg Waenhuiskrans Cave

De Mond

Struispunt De Mond Arniston1815
Reserve
Forest

Mond
t. Res.

Struis Bay

INDIAN

OCEAN

Oriental Pioneer 1974

Park

Five Mile Bank

N

Copyright © Map Studio MMI

20° 15' 20° 30'

ital or City ⊙ Other Town ▲ Place of Interest ✈ Major Airport Ⓣ Toll Route
jor Town ○ Settlement ★ Historical Site Airfield Ⓣ Toll Plaza
condary Town ⌂ Accommodation ◀ Border Control ▲ Major Spot Height Marsh

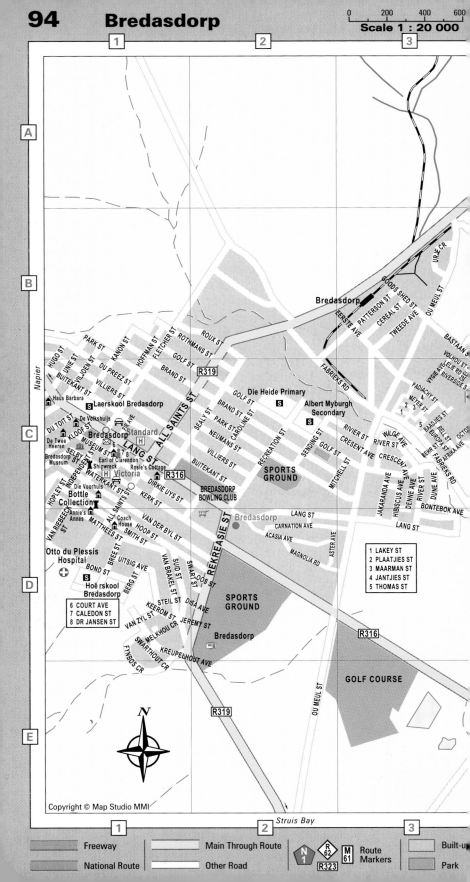

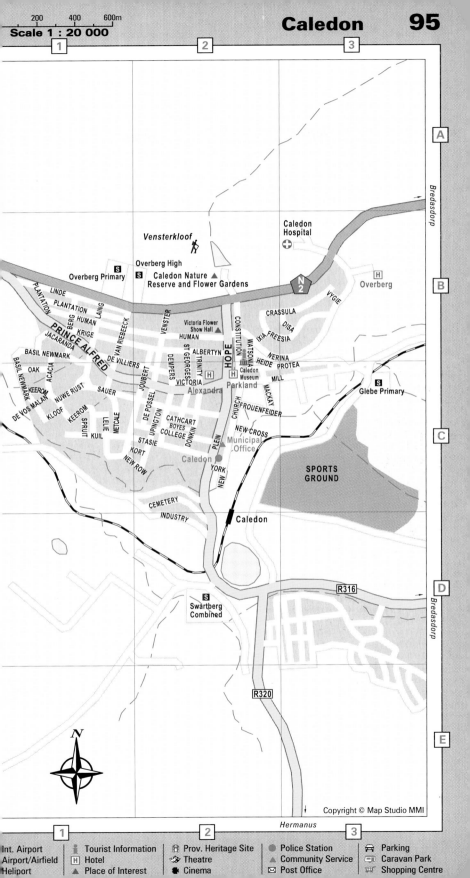

Scale 1 : 20 000

200 400 600m

1 **2** **3**

Bredasdorp

A

B

Bredasdorp

C

D

E

Vensterkloof

Caledon
Hospital

Overberg High
Overberg Primary

Caledon Nature
Reserve and Flower Gardens

N2

Overberg

CRASSULA

VYGIE

DISA

LINDE

PLANTATION

BERG HUMAN

KRIGE

LAING

PRINCE ALFRED

JACARANDA

BASIL NEWMARK

OAK

ACACIA

DE VILLIERS

VAN RIEBEECK

VENSTER

Victoria Flower
Show Hall

HUMAN

ST GEORGES

ALBERTYN

TRINITY

CONSTITUTION

HOPE

WATSON

HEIDE

NERINA

FREESIA

IXIA

PROTEA

KEEROM

NUWE RUST

SAUER

JOUBERT

DEMPERS

VICTORIA

Alexandra

Caledon
Museum

Parkland

MILL

MACKAY

Glebe Primary

BASIL NEWMARK

DE VOS MALAN

KLOOF

KEEROM

SPRUIT

LELIE

KUIL

METCALF

DE POSSEL

UPINGTON

CATHCART
BOYES
COLLEGE

STASIE

KORT

DOWNS

CHURCH

FROUENFEIDER

NEW CROSS

Municipal
Office

PLEIN

NEW ROW

Caledon

YORK

NEW

CEMETERY

INDUSTRY

Caledon

SPORTS
GROUND

R316

Swartberg
Combined

R320

N

Copyright © Map Studio MMI

Hermanus

Int. Airport
Airport/Airfield
Heliport

Tourist Information
H Hotel
Place of Interest

Prov. Heritage Site
Theatre
Cinema

Police Station
Community Service
Post Office

Parking
Caravan Park
Shopping Centre

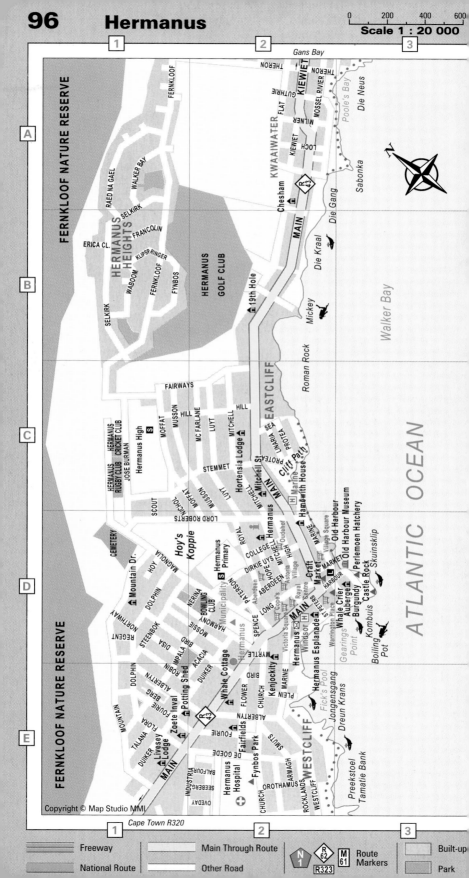

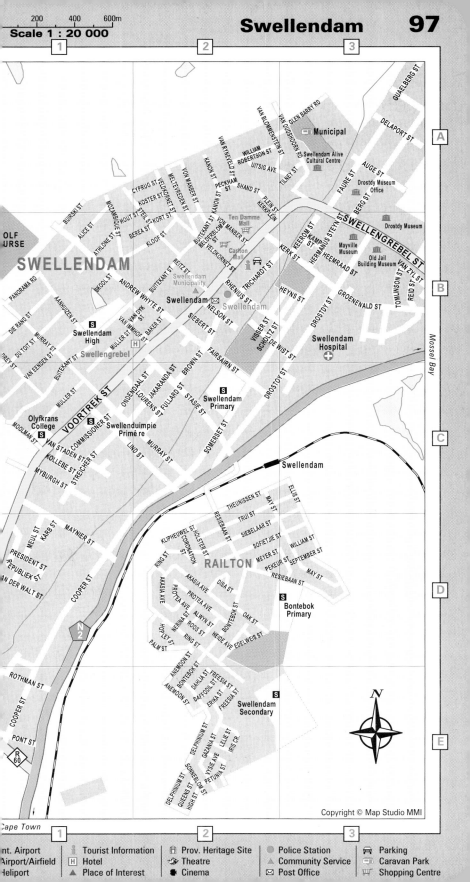

About 280-million years ago, when the earth was much younger, the Great Karoo was a vast swamp. Today, among the world's most fascinating arid zones, it is a place of infinite horizons and endless plains, rimmed by blue mountains. Visually, it is stark, but its very starkness distils into grandiose beauty that is often awesome. Sunsets and dawns stun with their vivid bursts of colour and cloud shows, while night skies are filled with stars you can almost touch.

STORM CLOUDS FORM OVER THE KAROO

The Karoo, the world's largest plateau outside Asia, is five times the size of Great Britain and considered a wonder of the scientific world. Its name comes from the indigenous word for thirstland. In South Africa it stands alone; globally the region is an envied rarity. Ancient and fossil-rich, the Karoo features the largest variety of succulents found anywhere on earth. Some of the world's most important archaeological and stone age sites are located in the Karoo. A rich legacy of rock art and artefacts makes it integral to the work of many scientists. A myriad species of indigenous and rare game roam these plains, while bird life is abundant.

Over a century ago, British soldiers, with all the paraphernalia of battle, moved across the plains of the Karoo to engage the Boers in the Anglo-Boer War. Now lonely graves dot these plains and the silent blockhouses still guard the railway lines as grim reminders of those turbulent times.

The Karoo is indeed a place of infinite enchantment and mystery. Those who linger in its vastness soon sense the magic and are drawn back again and again.

The Cape
South Africa
Western Cape Tourism Board
www.capetourism.org

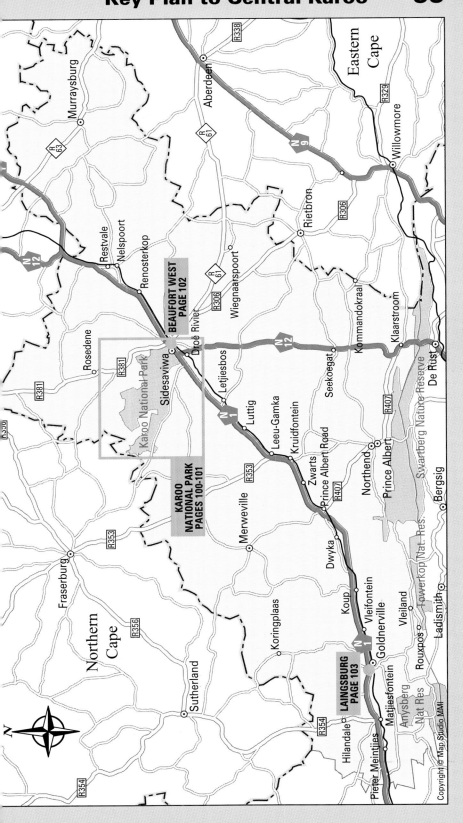

Eastern
Cape

Northern
Cape

**BEAUFORT WEST
PAGE 102**

**KAROO
NATIONAL PARK
PAGES 100-101**

**LAINGSBURG
PAGE 103**

Murraysburg

Aberdeen

Willowmore

Rietbron

Restvale

Nelspoort

Renosterkop

Droë Rivier

Wiegnaarspoort

Kommandokraal

Klaarstroom

De Rust

Rosedene

Sidesaviwa

Karoo National Park

Letjiesbos

Seekoegat

Swartberg Nature Reserve

Luttig

Leeu-Gamka

Kruidfontein

Prince Albert Road

Northend

Prince Albert

Bergsig

Zwarts

Fraserburg

Merweville

Dwyka

Towerkop Nat. Res.

Koringplaas

Koup

Vleifontein

Vleiland

Rouxpos

Ladismith

Sutherland

Goldnerville

Matjiesfontein

Hilandale

Pieter Meintjies

Anysberg
Nat Res

R338

R329

R63

R61

N9

R306

N12

R61

R306

R381

R381

R353

N1

R407

R353

R356

R354

R407

R354

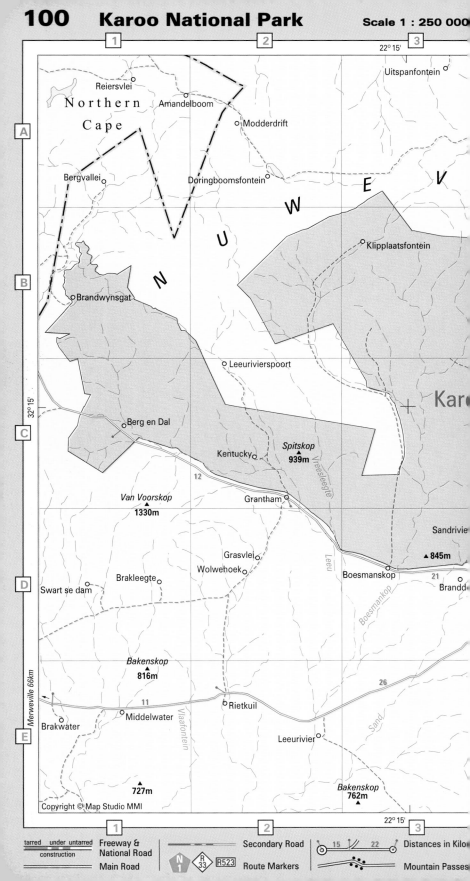

22° 15'

1 **2** **3**

A

Uitspanfontein

N o r t h e r n

Reiersvlei

Amandelboom

C a p e

Modderdrift

W

E

V

Bergvallei

Doringboomsfontein

U

Klipplaatsfontein

B

N

Brandwynsgat

32° 15'

Leeurivierspoort

Kar

C

Berg en Dal

12

Kentucky

Spitskop
▲ 939m

Vleesleegte

Van Voorskop
▲
1330m

Grantham

Sandrivie

Leeu

▲ 845m

Grasvlei

Wolwehoek

Boesmanskop

21

D

Swart se dam

Brakleegte

Brandd

Boesmanskop

Merweville 66km

Bakenskop
▲
816m

26

Sand

11

Rietkuil

Vlaafontein

E

Brakwater

Middelwater

Leeurivier

▲
727m

Bakenskop
762m
▲

Copyright © Map Studio MMI

22° 15'

1 **2** **3**

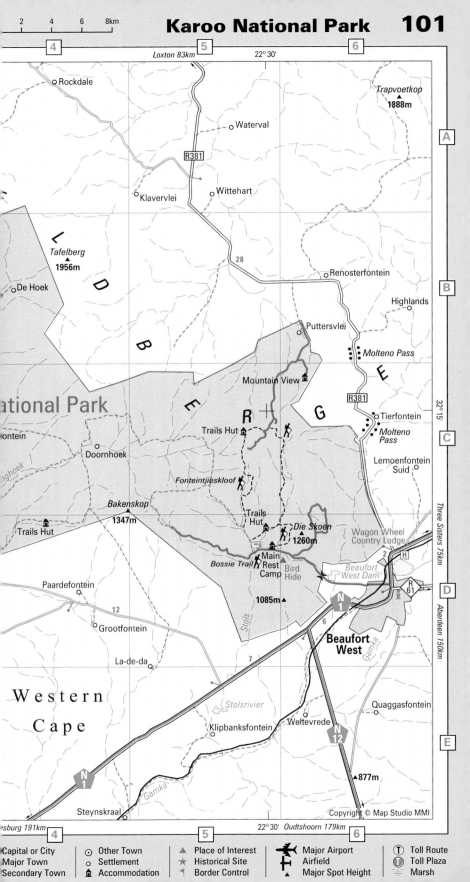

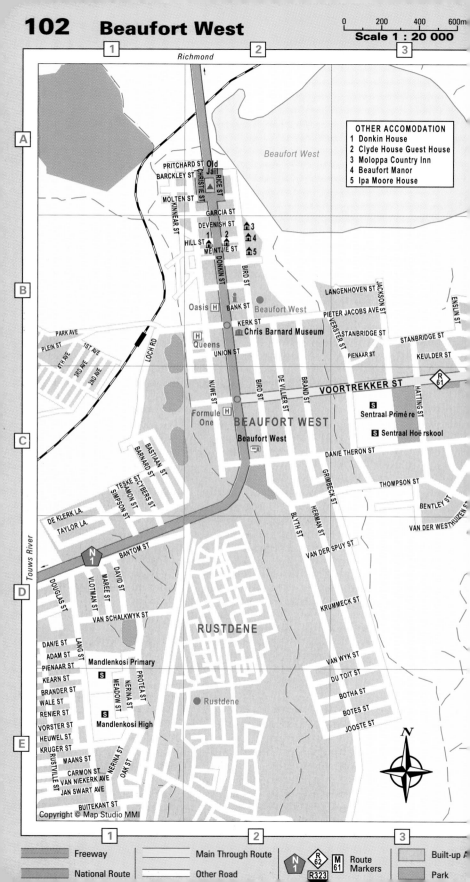

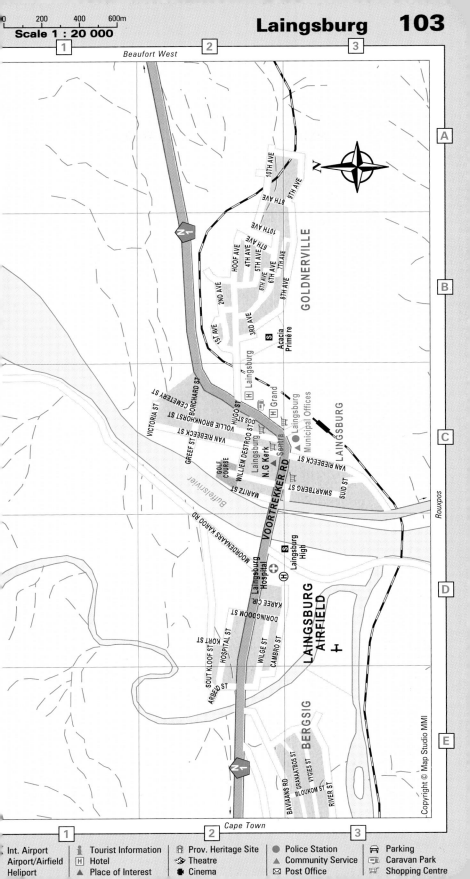

Scale 1 : 20 000

200   400   600m

1 Beaufort West **2** **3**

A

B

C

N↑1

GOLDNERVILLE

10TH AVE
9TH AVE
8TH AVE
10TH AVE
8TH AVE
HOOF AVE
4TH AVE
5TH AVE
7TH AVE
6TH AVE
6TH AVE
8TH AVE
2ND AVE
1ST AVE
3RD AVE

Acacia
Primère

Laingsburg

Grand

Laingsburg
Municipal Offices

LAINGSBURG

VAN RIEBEECK ST

BORCHARD ST
CEMETERY ST
VICTORIA ST
VOLLIE BRONKHORST ST
HUGO ST
OOS ST
GREEF ST
WILLIEM DESTROO ST
VAN RIEBEECK ST
Laingsburg
Sentra
N.G Kerk
GOLF
COURSE
MARITZ ST
SWARTBERG ST
SUID ST

VOORTREKKER RD

Buffelsrivier

MOORDENAARS KAROO RD

Laingsburg
High

Laingsburg
Hospital

LAINGSBURG
AIRFIELD

D

KAREE CIR.
DORINGBOOM ST
HOSPITAL ST
SOUT KLOOF ST
KORT ST
ARBED ST
WILGE ST
CAMBRO ST

BERGSIG

BAVIAANS RD
GRANAATBOS ST
VYGIES ST
BLOUKOM ST
RIVER ST

N↑1

E

Rouxpos

Copyright © Map Studio MMI

1 Cape Town **2** **3**

Int. Airport	Tourist Information	Prov. Heritage Site	Police Station	Parking
Airport/Airfield	Hotel	Theatre	Community Service	Caravan Park
Heliport	Place of Interest	Cinema	Post Office	Shopping Centre

The Klein Karoo Kannaland has a spectacular landscape fashioned almost entirely by water, with vegetation ranging from lush greenery in the fertile river valleys to short, rugged Karoo plants in the veld. Gorges follow rivers that cut through towering mountains, while breathtakingly steep passes cross imposing terrain. The long, narrow valley is rich in geological shapes, being home to the spectacular Cango Caves, a series of magnificent, glittering limestone caverns fashioned over millennia beneath the foothills of the Swartberg Range. The region also boasts many species of indigenous plants, and is the natural habitat of the largest bird in the world – the ostrich.

RIDING OSTRICHES IS A GREAT ATTRACTION

However, the region is also profoundly rich in culture and history. The annual Klein Karoo Kunstefees draws thousands of arts lovers to enjoy music, theatre and dance, while Bushman paintings offer a drawcard equally strong. A climate dominated by the sun produces excellent Port wines, honey-sweet fruits, raisins and cheese.

Three beautifully-set Mission Stations depict a quaint and unique architecture of a century ago, while attractive sandstone mansions, or Feather Palaces remind one of the heady days when the ostrich feather industry was at its peak. Oudtshoorn, the centre of the ostrich industry, has remained the region's leading town.

Sunny conditions inspire the region's popular pastimes, which include hiking, mountain-biking, 4x4 excursions, caving, climbing, horse riding, bird-watching, fishing and much, much more. The main road through the Klein Karoo Kannaland is the R62 – the Great Alternative Scenic Route – stretching from Cape Town via Worcester, Montagu and Oudtshoorn (approximately 4 hours) to the coast and Port Elizabeth.

The Cape
South Africa

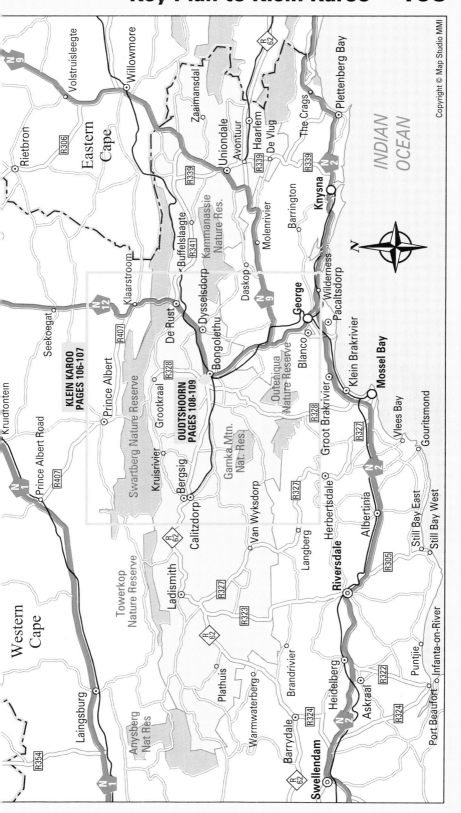

INDIAN OCEAN

Eastern Cape

Western Cape

KLEIN KAROO
PAGES 106-107

OUDTSHOORN
PAGES 108-109

Swartberg Nature Reserve

Towerkop
Nature Reserve

Anysberg
Nat Res

Gamka Mtn.
Nat. Res.

Outeniqua
Nature Reserve

Kammanassie
Nature Res.

Volstruisleegte
Willowmore
Zaaimansdal
Uniondale
Avontuur
Haarlem
De Vlug
The Crags
Plettenberg Bay
Rietbron
Knysna
Barrington
Molenrivier
Buffelslaagte
Klaarstroom
Daskop
George
Wilderness
Pacaltsdorp
De Rust
Dysselsdorp
Bongolethu
Blanco
Klein Brakrivier
Mossel Bay
Prince Albert
Grootkraal
Groot Brakrivier
Vlees Bay
Gouritsmond
Kruisrivier
Bergsig
Van Wyksdorp
Calitzdorp
Still Bay East
Still Bay West
Herbertsdale
Ladismith
Langberg
Riversdale
Albertinia
Langberg
Brandrivier
Plathuis
Puntjie
Infanta-on-River
Warmwaterberg
Brandrivier
Heidelberg
Askraal
Port Beaufort
Laingsburg
Barrydale
Swellendam
Kruidfontein
Prince Albert Road
Seekoegat
Seekoegat

N9
N12
N9
N2
N1
N2
N2
N1

R306
R339
R341
R328
R407
R327
R328
R327
R323
R62
R62
R62
R62
R305
R322
R324
R324
R354
R339
R339
R62

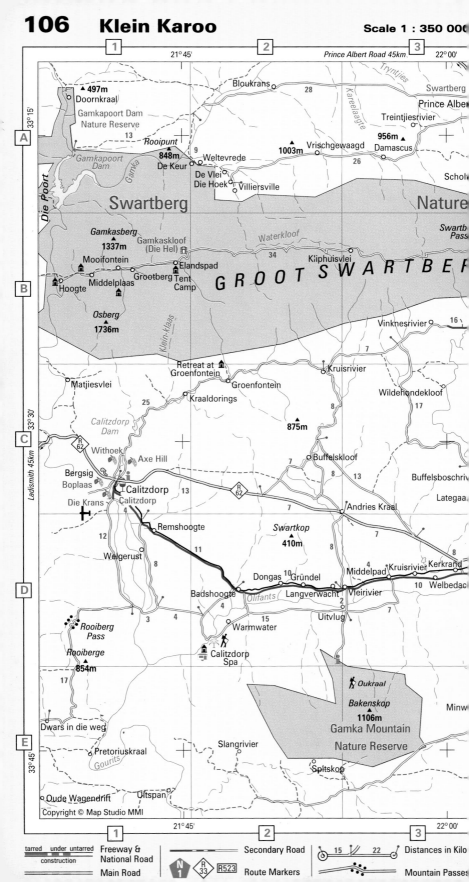

Prince Albert Road 45km

1   21° 45'   **2**   22° 00'   **3**

Tryntjies

Swartberg

Prince Albe

▲ 497m
Doornkraal
Gamkapoort Dam
Nature Reserve

Bloukrans

28

Kareelaagte

Treintjiesrivier

A   33° 15'

13

Gamkapoort
Dam

Rooipunt

▲ 848m
De Keur

Weltevrede

De Vlei
Die Hoek

Villiersville

956m ▲

1003m ▲ Vrischgewaagd

Damascus

Schol

9

26

Gamka

Swartberg

Nature

Die Poort

Waterkloof

Swartb
Pass

Gamkasberg
▲
1337m

Gamkaskloof
(Die Hel)

Elandspad

Mooifontein

Grootberg Tent
Camp

34

Kliphuisvlei

B

Hoogte

Middelplaas

G R O O T   S W A R T B E R

Osberg
▲
1736m

Klein-Klaas

Vinknesrivier

16

7

Retreat at
Groenfontein

Kruisrivier

Wildehondekloof

Matjiesvlei

25

Groenfontein

Kraaldorings

17

8

Calitzdorp
Dam

875m ▲

C   33° 30'

Withoek

Axe Hill

Buffelskloof

7

Buffelsboschriv

Bergsig
Boplaas

R
62

Calitzdorp

8

13

Lategaa

Die Krans

Calitzdorp

13

R
62

Andries Kraal

Ladismith 45km

4

Remshoogte

Swartkop
▲
410m

7

8

Kerkrand

12

11

8

Welgerust

Middelpad

Kruisrivier

8

8

Dongas

Gründel

4

Welbedac

D

3

4

Badshoogte

Olifants

10

Langverwacht

Vleirivier

10

2

7

Warmwater

15

Uitvlug

Rooiberg
Pass

4

Calitzdorp
Spa

Oukraal

Rooiberge
▲
854m

Bakenskop
▲
1106m

Minw

17

Gamka Mountain

E   33° 45'

Dwars in die weg

Slangrivier

Nature Reserve

Pretoriuskraal

Gourits

Spitskop

Oude Wagendrift

Uitspan

21° 45'   **1**   **2**   **3**   22° 00'

tarred   under   untarred
     construction

Freeway &
National Road

Main Road

N
1

R
33

R523

Secondary Road

Route Markers

15   22

Distances in Kilo

Mountain Passes

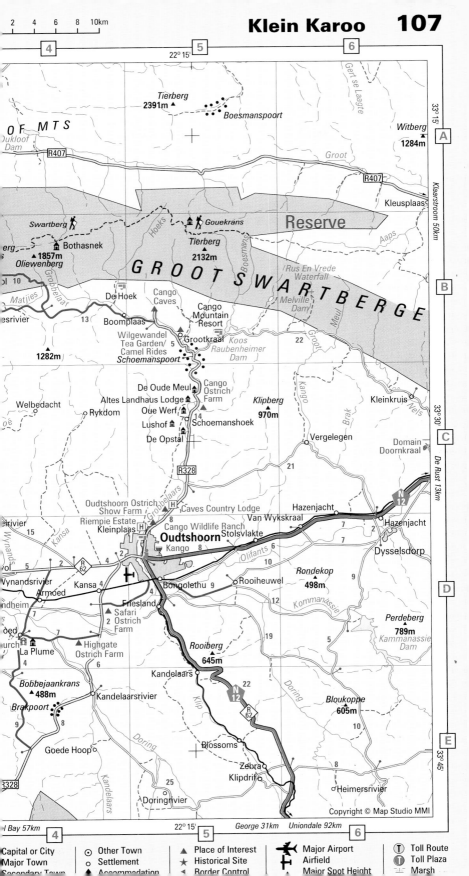

Map labels:

2 4 6 8 10km

22° 15'

OF MTS

Dukloof Dam

R407

Tierberg 2391m

Boesmanspoort

Witberg 1284m

Klaarstroom 50km

33° 15' A

Groot

R407

Kleusplaas

Swartberg

Bothasnek 1857m

Oliewenberg

berg

Hoeks

Gouekrans

Tierberg 2132m

Boesmans

Reserve

Aaps

Rus En Vrede Waterfall

Melville Dam

Meul

Groot

33° 30' B

GROOT SWARTBERGE

Matjies

esrivier

13

De Hoek

Boomplaas

Cango Caves

Cango Mountain Resort

Wilgewandel Tea Garden/ Camel Rides

Grootkraal

Koos Raubenheimer Dam

5

22

1282m

Schoemanspoort

De Oude Meul

Altes Landhaus Lodge

Cango Ostrich Farm

Klipberg 970m

Kleinkruis

Nels

Welbedacht

Rykdom

Oue Werf

Lushof

De Opstal

14

Schoemanshoek

Kango

Brak

Vergelegen

Domain Doornkraal

De Rust 13km

33° 30' C

R328

21

oe

eirivier

15

Oudtshoorn Ostrich Show Farm

Riempie Estate

Kleinplaas

Grobbelaars

Caves Country Lodge

Cango Wildlife Ranch

Kango

Hazenjacht

Van Wykskraal

8

Stolsvlakte

7

N12

2

Hazenjacht

Dysselsdorp

33° 30'

Kansa

Wynandsrivier

5

R62

4

2

Oudtshoorn

8

Olifants

6

10

7

Rondekop 498m

9

D

Vynandsrivier

Armoed

Kansa

4

Bongolethu

9

Rooiheuwel

Kommanassie

12

Perdeberg 789m

Kammanassie Dam

ndheim

7

Friesland

Safari Ostrich Farm

2

19

5

oed

urch

7

La Plume

Highgate Ostrich Farm

4

6

Rooiberg 645m

Kandelaars

Doring

Klip

N12 22

Bloukoppe 605m

33° 45' E

Bobbejaankrans 488m

Brakpoort

9

8

Kandelaarsrivier

R62

10

Goede Hoop

Doring

Blossoms

Kandelaars

Zebra

Klipdrif

Heimersrivier

8

3328

25

Doringrivier

22° 15'

George 31km Uniondale 92km

l Bay 57km

Legend:

Capital or City

Other Town

Place of Interest

Major Airport

Toll Route

Major Town

Settlement

Historical Site

Airfield

Toll Plaza

Secondary Town

Accommodation

Border Control

Major Spot Height

Marsh

200 400 600m

4 5 6

A

BONGOLETHU

George

Oudtshoorn

B

N 12

Best Little

LANGENHOVEN RD

BRIDGTON

Protea

Laerskool
Bergsig

Protea Primary

Hoërskool
Morester

Laerskool
Van Rheede
Primary

HIG

COW

Junior Primary

Laerskool
Westbank

WESTBANK

SPORTS GROUND

SCHOOL
SPORTS
GROUND

Grobbelaars

SHOWGROUND

N 12

R 62

Petra
Meieskool

C

RAUBENHEIMER DR.

KEYTER ST

Raubenheimer Dr.

D

JAN VAN RIEBEECK RD

BUITENKANT ST

PARK RD

OUDTSHOORN
AIRPORT

E

Copyright © Map Studio MMI

Calitzdorp

4 5 6

To many who have visited it, the Garden Route has a mysterious allure. A most unusual part of Africa, it is also the sunny corner of the Cape where evergreen forests, verdant fields, tranquil inland lakes, sparkling bays and pristine beaches languish in a sultry climate. Stretching along the southern Cape Coast from Heidelberg in the west to the Tsitsikamma Forest and Storms River in the east, the region's entrance to the interior is barred by towering mountains breached by breathtaking passes and gorges. The silence evoked by its ever-changing landscape carries on its still, fragrant, sea-scented air a sense of the spiritual. With so much of the Garden Route's beauty unspoilt, visitors may feel they have been set free to play in God's back yard.

A well-developed tourist infrastructure has strung the region's towns along its coast like a string of pearls. In all of them, artists, writers, naturalists and nature lovers co-exist with those devoting their time and energies to catering to the whims and fancies of the area's year-round visitors. This is where the Outeniqua Choo-Tjoe still steams its way between George and Knysna every day. Whales come to calve and mate in the many

THE OUTENIQUA "CHOO TJOE" CROSSES THE KAAIMANS RIVER

unspoiled bays. Importantly, the area boasts two national parks – Tsitsikamma and Wilderness – as well as numerous other provincial and private nature reserves.

A treasure trove of history, culture, food, sport and entertainment awaits you between Heidelberg and Plettenberg Bay. Indeed, the Garden Route is a veritable playground, offering every sport imaginable – from golf to scuba-diving, abseiling to mountain biking. Beyond this, there are those unforgettable wild and lonely reaches that will touch your soul and revive your spirit.

TheCape

South Africa

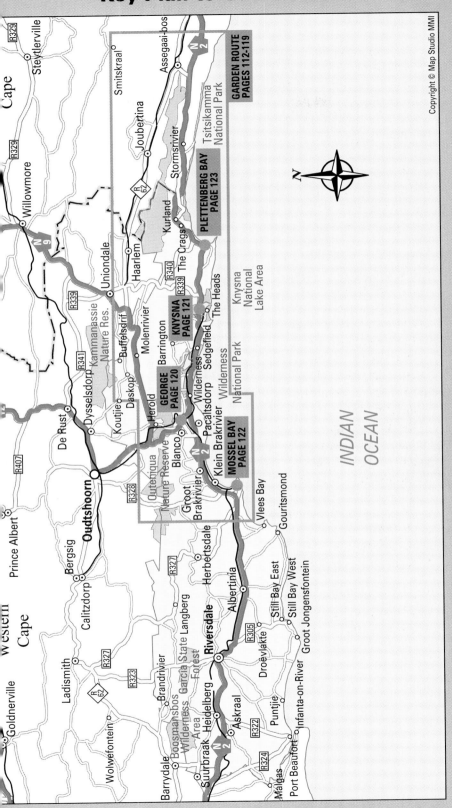

Cape

Steytlerville

R329

R329

Willowmore

N9

Smitskraal

Assegaai-bos

N2

Joubertina

Stormsrivier

Tsitsikamma
National Park

**GARDEN ROUTE
PAGES 112-119**

N

Kurland

The Crags

**PLETTENBERG BAY
PAGE 123**

R62

Uniondale

Haarlem

R340

R339

The Heads

Knysna
National
Lake Area

Kammanassie
Nature Res.

R339

Buffelsdrif

Molenrivier

**KNYSNA
PAGE 121**

Barrington

R341

Dysselsdorp

Koutjie

Daskop

Herold

**GEORGE
PAGE 120**

Wilderness

Sedgefield

Wilderness
National Park

De Rust

R407

Outeniqua
Nature Reserve

Blanco

Pacaltsdorp

Prince Albert

Bergsig

Oudtshoorn

R328

Klein Brakrivier

**MOSSEL BAY
PAGE 122**

Groot
Brakrivier

Vlees Bay

Gouritsmond

Calitzdorp

R327

Herbertsdale

INDIAN
OCEAN

Ladismith

R62

R327

R323

Brandrivier

Garcia State
Forest

Langberg

Albertinia

Riversdale

Still Bay East

Still Bay West

Groot Jongensfontein

Goldnerville

Boosmansbos
Wilderness
Area

Heidelberg

Droëvlakte

R305

Wolwefontein

Barrydale

Suurbraak

Askraal

Puntjie

Infanta-on-River

N2

R322

Port Beaufort

Malgas

R324

Western
Cape

Western
Cape

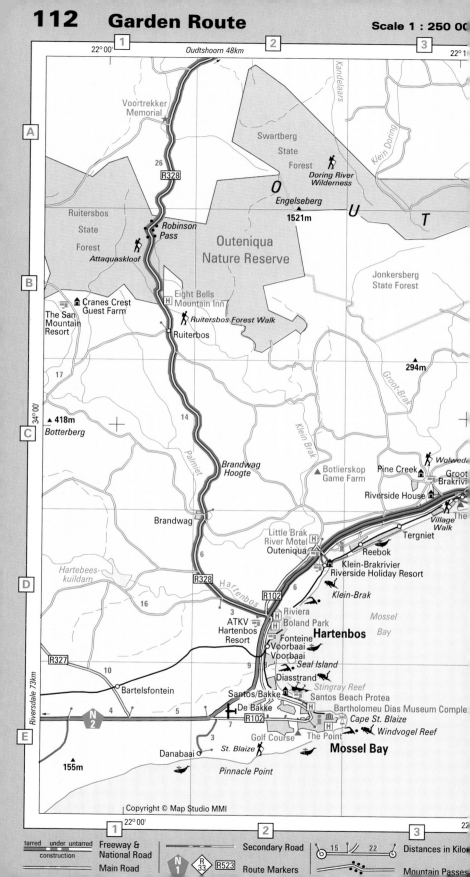

2 4 6 8km

4 5 6

Oudtshoorn 41km 22° 30'

R 62
7
Holgate
N 12
Perdepoort 1214m Eseljagpoort 10 R 62
N 9
Camfer Eseljag
Herold
9
Doring River Langkloof State Forest Pass to Pass Oupad A
Waboomskraal 18 Montagu Pass and Old Smithy Topping Cradocks Peak U Outeniqua Nature Reserve
Highlands Lodge N 9
Montagu 1579m Witfontein State Forest
1374m N Outeniqua Pass Pass George Peak Outeniqua Groeneweide Forest Trails
Saagtandberg 1337m Q
Witfontein State Forest Old Toll House Garden Route Dam
Power Swart 10 Saasveld
B
Fancourt Manor House Hawthorndene George Museum (Old Drostdy) Stone Bridge 6
Blanco N 12 H 4 GEORGE Far Hills Protea Wilderness
Fancourt Hotel and Country Club Estate Golf Course Gateway Kaaimans 40km 34° 00'
Bado Kidogo King George III Old Slave Tree Outeniqua Lodge H
R 404 George Tourist Resort Railway 2 Fairy Knowe
R 102 3 Brigadoon Park Sea Glimpse Holiday Resort Victoria Bay H
9 Gwaing Delville Park Carmel by the Sea Victoria Bay
GEORGE Mission Church Skuinsbank C
N 2 Pacaltsdorp
Outeniqua Skimmelkrans Rooiklip
Glentana Beach Walks Herolds Bay Dolphin View Kwelanga Lodge
Rock 8 Herold's Bay Herolds Bay
ana 1902 Glentana The Cave Voëlklip Oubaai
Ghwanobaai

🏠 IN THE VICTORIA BAY AREA
Ballots Bay Coastal Lodge
Island Lake Resort
Seabreeze Holiday Cabanas
The Waves
Victoria Bay Lodge

N

INDIAN

OCEAN

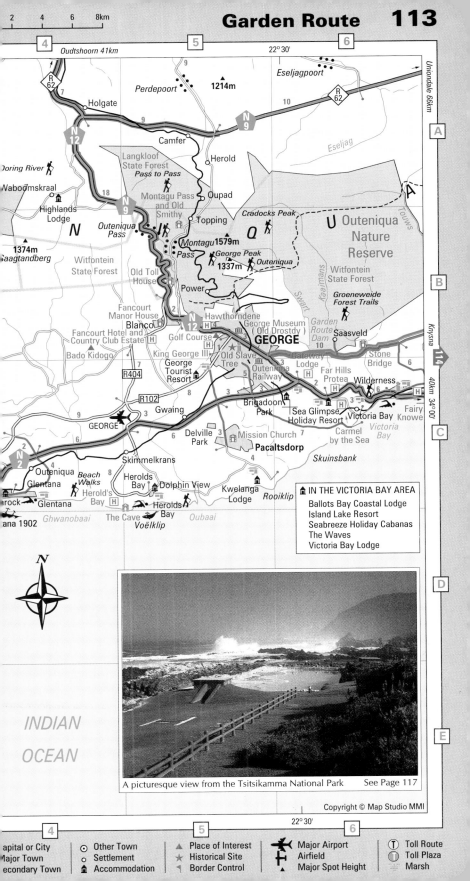
A picturesque view from the Tsitsikamma National Park See Page 117

22° 30'

4 5 6

apital or City ⊙ Other Town ▲ Place of Interest ✈ Major Airport Ⓣ Toll Route
Major Town ○ Settlement ★ Historical Site Airfield Ⓣ Toll Plaza
econdary Town ▲ Accommodation Border Control Major Spot Height Marsh

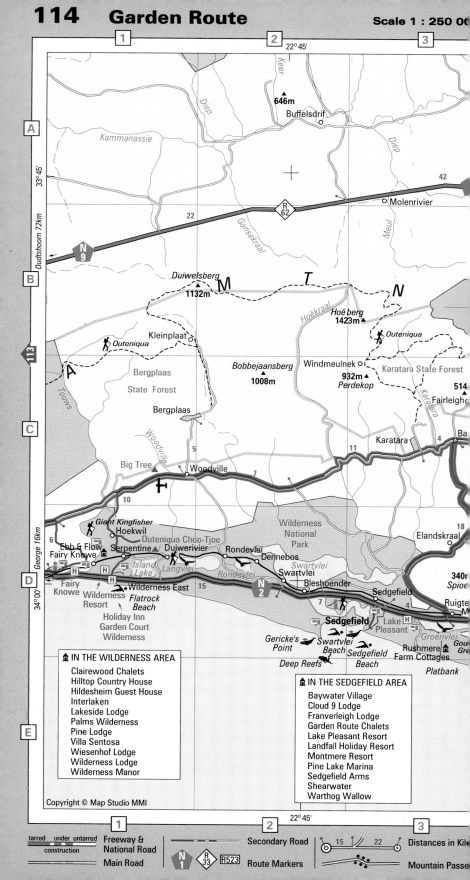

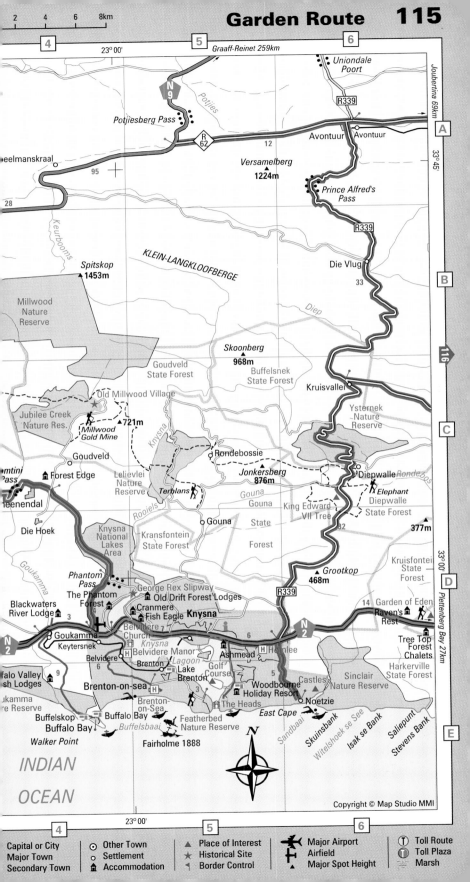

Graaff-Reinet 259km

Joubertina 69km

Uniondale Poort

R339

Potjiesberg Pass

R62

Avontuur
Avontuur

Versamelberg
1224m

Prince Alfred's Pass

R339

KLEIN-LANGKLOOFBERGE

Spitskop
1453m

Die Vlug

Diep

Millwood
Nature
Reserve

Keurbooms

Skoonberg
968m

Goudveld
State Forest

Buffelsnek
State Forest

Kruisvallei

Old Millwood Village

Jubilee Creek
Nature Res.

Millwood
Gold Mine
721m

Ysternek
Nature
Reserve

Goudveld

Knysna

Rondebossie

Lelievlei
Nature
Reserve

Jonkersberg
876m

Diepwalle
Rondeb

mtini
Pass

Forest Edge

Terblans

Elephant
Diepwalle
State Forest

eenendal

Die Hoek

Rooiels

Gouna

Gouna

Gouna

King Edward
VII Tree

377m

Knysna
National Lakes
Area

Kransfontein
State Forest

State

Kruisfontei
State
Forest

Phantom
Pass

Grootkop
468m

Goukamma

The Phantom
Forest

George Rex Slipway

Old Drift Forest Lodges

R339

Garden of Eden

Blackwaters
River Lodge

Cranmere
Fish Eagle

Knysna

Raven's
Rest

Tree Top
Forest
Chalets

N2

Goukamma
Keytersnek

Belvidere
Church

Belvidere Manor

Ashmead

Hornlee

N2

Belvidere

Brenton

Knysna
Lagoon

Lake
Brenton

Golf
Course

Sinclair
Nature Reserve

Harkerville
State Forest

falo Valley
sh Lodges

Brenton-on-sea

Brenton-
on-Sea

Woodbourne
Holiday Resort

Castles

ukamma
re Reserve

Buffelskop
Buffalo Bay

Buffalo Bay

Featherbed
Nature Reserve

The Heads

East Cape

Noetzie

Skuinsbank

Isak se Bank

Saliepunt
Stevens Bank

Walker Point

Buffelsbaai

Fairholme 1888

Witelshoek se See

Sandbaai

INDIAN

OCEAN

23° 00'

Copyright © Map Studio MMI

Capital or City	⊙ Other Town	▲ Place of Interest	✈ Major Airport	Ⓣ Toll Route
Major Town	⊙ Settlement	★ Historical Site	Airfield	Ⓣ Toll Plaza
Secondary Town	⌂ Accommodation	◁ Border Control	▲ Major Spot Height	Marsh

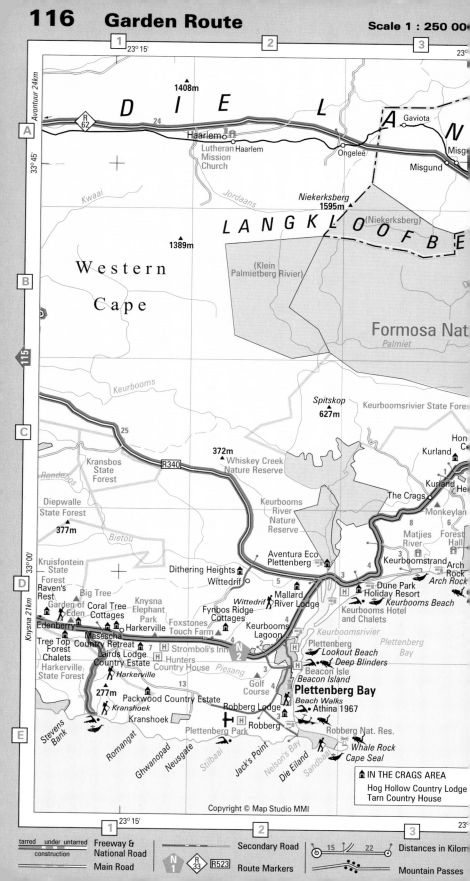

D I E **L A**

L A N G K L O O F B E

Western Cape

Formosa Nat

1408m

R 62

24

Haarlemo

Lutheran Haarlem
Mission Church

Gaviota

Ongeleë

Misg

Misgund

Kwaai

Jordaans

Niekerksberg
1595m

(Niekerksberg)

1389m

(Klein
Palmietberg Rivier)

Palmiet

Avontuur 24km

33° 45'

Keurbooms

Spitskop
627m

Keurboomsrivier State Fores

25

R340

372m
Whiskey Creek
Nature Reserve

Kurland

Kurland

The Crags

Monkeylan

Kransbos
State
Forest

Rondebos

Keurbooms
River
Nature
Reserve

Matjies
River

Forest
Hall

Diepwalle
State Forest

Bietou

377m

Keurboomstrand

Arch
Rock

Arch Rock

Kruisfontein
State
Forest

Raven's
Rest

Big Tree

Garden of
Eden

Coral Tree
Cottages

Knysna
Elephant
Park

Dithering Heights

Wittedrif

Wittedrif

Aventura Eco
Plettenberg

Mallard
River Lodge

Dune Park
Holiday Resort

Keurbooms Beach

Keurbooms Hotel
and Chalets

Edenberry

Masescha
Country Retreat

Harkerville

Foxstones
Touch Farm

Fynbos Ridge
Cottages

Keurbooms
Lagoon

Keurboomsrivier

Plettenberg

Plettenberg
Bay

Tree Top
Forest
Chalets

Lairds Lodge
Country Estate

Harkerville

Stromboli's Inn

Hunters
Country House

Piesang

Lookout Beach

Deep Blinders

Beacon Isle
Beacon Island

Harkerville
State
Forest

277m

Packwood Country Estate

Kranshoek

Kranshoek

13

Golf
Course

Plettenberg Bay

Beach Walks
Athina 1967

Knysna 21km

33° 00'

Stevens
Bank

Romangat

Ghwanopad

Neusgate

Robberg Lodge

Plettenberg Park

Robberg

Robberg Nat. Res.

Whale Rock
Cape Seal

Jack's Point

Nelson's Bay

Die Eiland

Sandbaai

Stilbaai

IN THE CRAGS AREA
Hog Hollow Country Lodge
Tarn Country House

Copyright © Map Studio MMI

tarred   under   untarred
    construction

**Freeway &
National Road**

Main Road

Secondary Road

Route Markers

N 1 / N 2   R 33   R523

15   22

Distances in Kilom

Mountain Passes

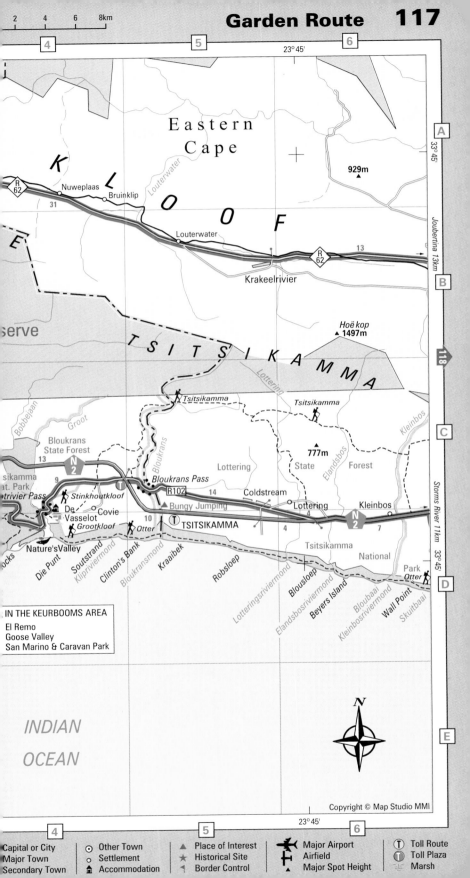

2 4 6 8km

4 5 6

23° 45'

Eastern Cape

K L O O F

R 62

Nuweplaas
Bruinklip

31

Louterwater

Louterwater

R 62 13

Krakeelrivier

929m ▲

Joubertina 13km

A

33° 45'

B

118

Hoë kop
▲ 1497m

T S I T S I K A M M A

Lottering

serve

Bobbejaan

Groot

Tsitsikamma

Tsitsikamma

Kleinbos

Bloukrans

C

Bloukrans
State Forest

777m ▲

Lottering

State

Forest

Elandsbos

Kleinbos

Storms River 11km

13

N
2

9

Bloukrans Pass

R102

14

Coldstream

Kleinbos

sikamma
Nat. Park
rivier Pass

Stinkhoutkloof

De
Vasselot Covie

Bungy Jumping

Lottering

4

N
2

7

Grootkloof

Otter

10

T TSITSIKAMMA

33° 45'

Nature's Valley

Soutstrand

Clinton's Bank

Kraaibek

Robsloep

Tsitsikamma

National

Park
Otter

D

Die Punt

Kliprivermond

Bloukransmond

Lotteringsriviermond

Blousloep

Beyers Island

Wall Point

Skuitbaai

Elandsbosriviermond

Bloubaai

Kleinbosriviermond

IN THE KEURBOOMS AREA
El Remo
Goose Valley
San Marino & Caravan Park

INDIAN

OCEAN

N

Copyright © Map Studio MMI

Capital or City	⊙ Other Town	▲ Place of Interest
Major Town	○ Settlement	★ Historical Site
Secondary Town	🏠 Accommodation	Border Control

Major Airport
Airfield
Major Spot Height

T Toll Route
Toll Plaza
Marsh

Scale 1 : 250 00

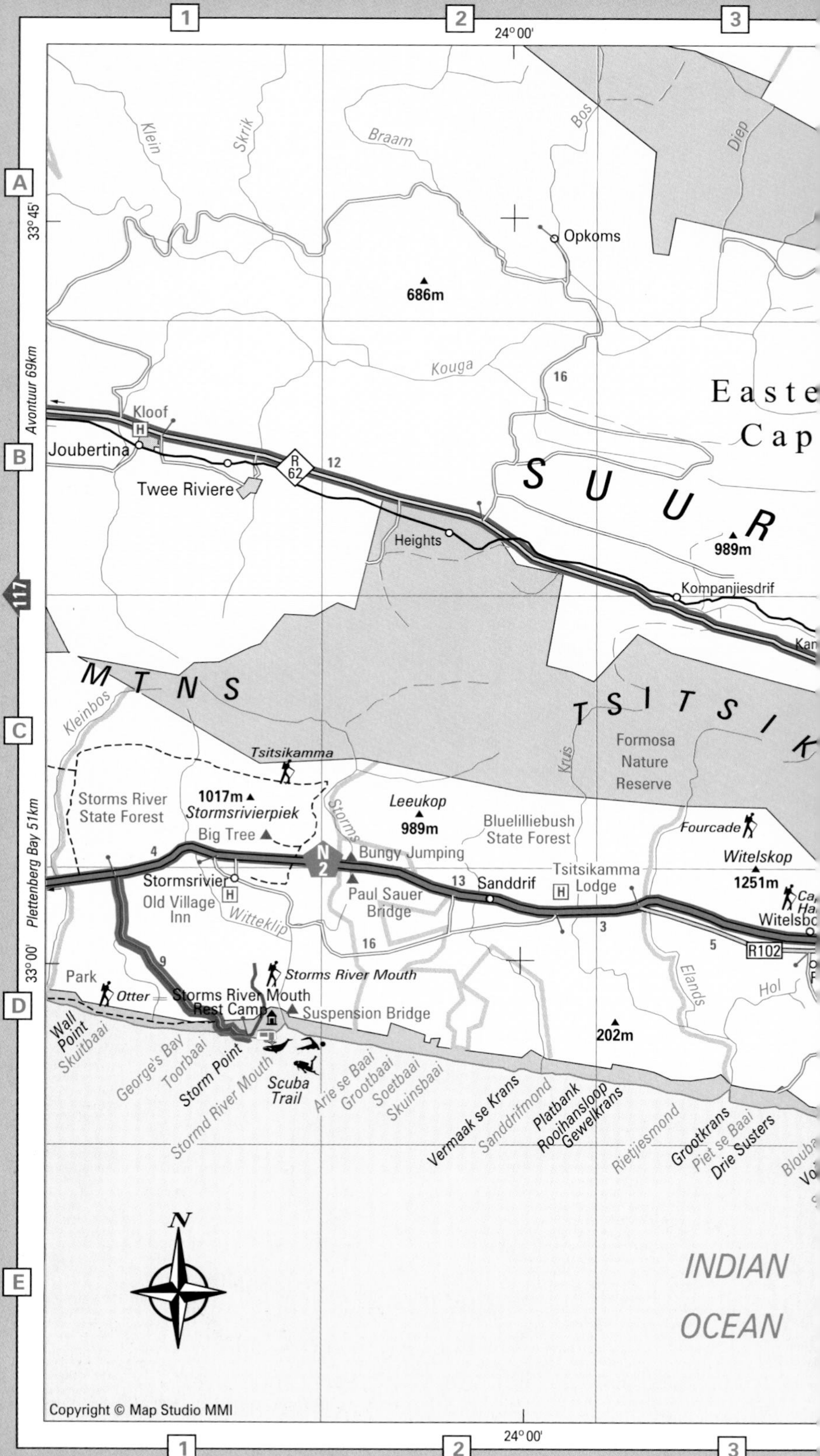

tarred under construction untarred Freeway & National Road

Main Road

Secondary Road

N 1 R 33 R523 Route Markers

15 22 Distances in Kil

Mountain Passe

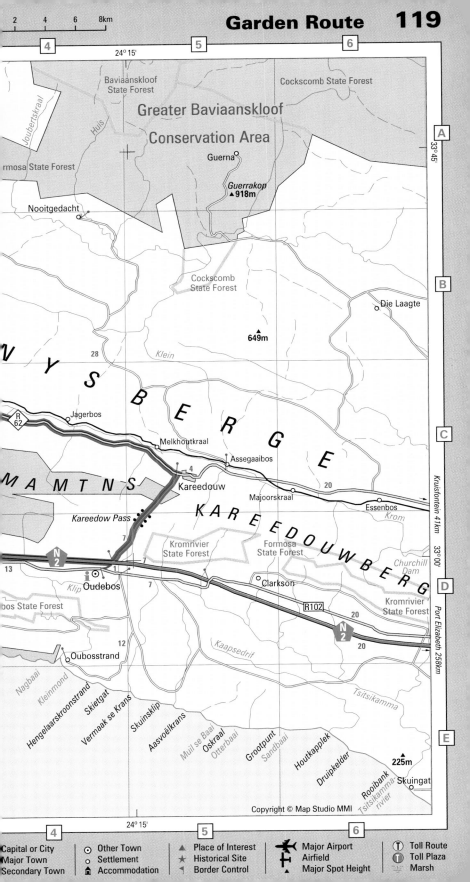

2 4 6 8km

4 24° 15' 5 6

Baviaanskloof
State Forest

Cockscomb State Forest

Greater Baviaanskloof

A

Conservation Area

Guerna

rmosa State Forest

Guerrakop
▲918m

Nooitgedacht

33° 45'

Cockscomb
State Forest

B

Die Laagte

▲649m

Klein

28

B
E
R
G
E

V
Y
S
B
E
R
G
E

R
62

Jagerbos

C

Melkhoutkraal

Assegaaibos

4

Kareedouw

Majoorskraal

20

Essenbos

Krom

M A M T N S

K
A
R
E
E
D
O
U
W
B
E
R
G

Kareedow Pass

7

Kromrivier
State Forest

Formosa
State Forest

Churchill
Dam

N
2

7

13

7

1

Klip

i

Oudebos

Clarkson

R102

Kromrivier
State Forest

D

33° 00'

Kruisfontein 41km

Port Elizabeth 258km

20

N
2

20

12

Oubosstrand

Kaapsedrif

bos State Forest

Nagbaai

Kleinmond

Hengelaarskroonstrand

Skietgat

Vermaak se Krans

Skuinsklip

Aasvoëlkrans

Muil se Baai

Oskraal

Otterbaai

Grootpunt

Sandbaai

Houtkapplek

Druipkelder

▲225m

Skuingat

Rooibank

Tsitsikamma
rivier

Tsitsikamma

E

Copyright © Map Studio MMI

24° 15'

4 5 6

Capital or City   ⊙ Other Town   ▲ Place of Interest   ✈ Major Airport   Ⓣ Toll Route
Major Town   ○ Settlement   ★ Historical Site   Airfield   Ⓣ Toll Plaza
Secondary Town   🏠 Accommodation   ◀ Border Control   Major Spot Height   Marsh

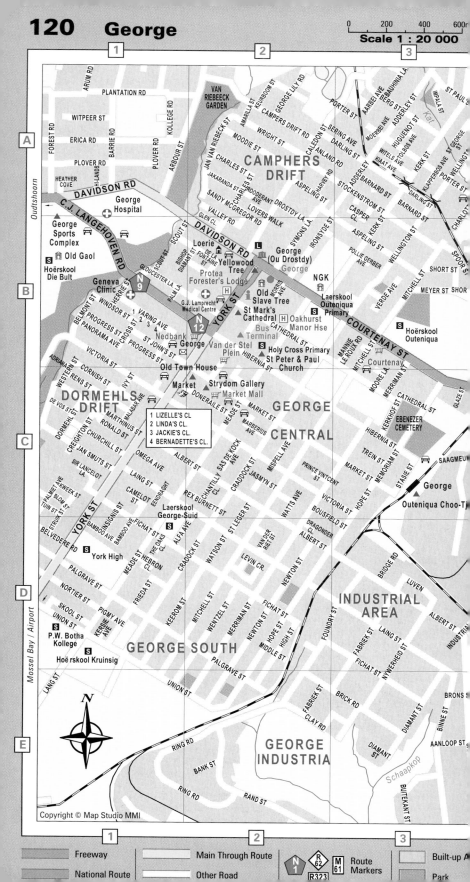

200   400   600

Oudtshoorn

Mossel Bay / Airport

A

B

C

D

E

1

2

3

PLANTATION RD
ARUM RD
WITPEER ST
ERICA RD
BARRIE RD
PLOVER RD
KOLLEGE RD
PLOVER RD
FOREST RD
HEATHER COVE
DAVIDSON RD
C.J. LANGEHOVEN RD
George Hospital
George Sports Complex
Old Gaol
Hoërskool Die Bult
Geneva Clinic
N 9
Kemferkie S.S.
WINDSOR ST
BELMONT RD
PROGRESS ST
PANORAMA AVE
VICTORIA ST
VARING AVE
PALM LA
GLOUCESTER LA
BISHOP DIAMANT ST
PROGRESS ST
ST JOHN'S ST
DORMEHLS DRIFT
DE VOS ST
ADRIAAN ST
WESTERN ST
RENS ST
CORNISH ST
MARTHINUS ST
RONALD ST
CHURCHILL ST
CREIGHTON ST
JAN SMUTS ST
MALABAR AVE
SIR LANCELOT LA
OMEGA AVE
CAMELOT ST
LAING ST
EINDRAGHT
ALBERT ST
INSIGNIS ST
BAMBOO AVE
PALMIET AVE
ZEEWEEK ST
BLOM ST
TUIN ST
STRUIS ST
BELVEDERE ST
PALGRAVE ST
York High
NORTIER ST
SKOOL ST
UNION ST
P.W. Botha Kollege
Hoërskool Kruinsig
GEORGE SOUTH
LANG ST
PIGMY AVE
KERSIE AVE
KEEROM ST
FRIEDA ST
THE OAKS
ST HEBRON CL.
MEADE ST
CRADOCK ST
ALFA AVE
FICHAT ST
BAMBOO AVE
Laerskool George-Suid
REX BURNETT ST
ST LEGER ST
WATSON ST
MITCHELL ST
WENTZEL ST
MERRIMAN ST
NEWTON ST
HOPE ST
HIGH ST
MIDDLE ST
PALGRAVE ST
UNION ST
RING RD
BANK ST
RING RD
RAND ST
CLAY RD
FABRIEK ST
BRICK RD
GEORGE INDUSTRIA
Schaapkop

VAN RIEBEECK GARDEN
AMARILLA ST
KEURBOOM ST
GEORGE LILY RD
CAMPERS DRIFT RD
WRIGHT ST
MOODIE ST
JAN VAN RIEBECK ST
CHARLES ST
JAKARANDA ST
GROODERANT DROSTDY AVE
SANDY MCGREGOR RD
GLEN LA
VALLEY RD
LOVERS WALK
DAVIDSON RD
Loerie
DE LA FONTAINE
Yellowwood Tree
Protea Forester's Lodge
G.J. Lamprecht Medical Centre
SYMONS LA
Old Slave Tree
St Mark's Cathedral
Oakhurst Manor Hse
Bus Terminal
Van der Stel Plein
George
Old Town House
Market
Strydom Gallery
Market Mall
DONERAILE ST
MEADE ST
MARBERIUS ST
MARKET ST
CAMPERS DRIFT RD
CALEDON ST
AANLAND RD
DARLING ST
SERING AVE
PORTER ST
ASPELING ST
MARKET ST
STOCKENSTROM ST
IRONSYDE ST
L
George (Ou Drostdy)
George
NGK
Laerskool Outeniqua Primary
CATHEDRAL ST
HIBERNIA ST
Holy Cross Primary
St Peter & Paul Church
DONERAILE ST
1 LIZELLE'S CL.
2 LINDA'S CL.
3 JACKIE'S CL.
4 BERNADETTE'S CL.
SAS DE KOCK AVE
CRADOCK ST
JASMYN ST
GEORGE CENTRAL
ALBERT ST
MISPELL AVE
PRINCE VINTCENT ST
VICTORIA ST
WATTS AVE
BOUSFIELD ST
DRAGONDER ST
ALBERT ST
VAN DER RIET ST
LEVIN CR.
NEWTON ST
FICHAT ST

AARBEI AVE
BAUHINIA ST
BERG ST
ADDERLEY ST
IMPALA ST
ST PAUL'S
MOERBEI AVE
HUGUENOT ST
TOLBOS AVE
KLAPPERBOS AVE
PORTER ST
WELLINGTON
ADDERLEY ST
WITELS AVE
KIAAT AVE
KERK ST
BARNARD ST
DARLING ST
ADDERLEY ST
BARNARD ST
CASPER CL
KERK ST
POLLIE GERBER AVE
ASPELING ST
WELLINGTON ST
VERDE AVE
SHORT ST
MITCHELL ST
MEYER ST
SHORT
COURTENAY ST
MANNIE LE ROUX RD
MITCHELL ST
MOORE LA
Courtenay
Hoërskool Outeniqua
MERRIMAN ST
HIBERNIA ST
TREIN ST
MARKET ST
MEMORIAM ST
EBENEZER CEMETERY
CATHEDRAL ST
KERKHOF ST
GLAZE ST
SAAGMEU
STASIE ST
George
Outeniqua Choo-Tj
HOPE ST
BRIDGE RD
LUVEN
ALBERT ST
INDUSTRIAL AREA
LAING ST
FABRIEK ST
NYWERHEID ST
FICHAT ST
FOUNDRY ST
INDUSTRIA
DIAMANT ST
BINNE ST
BRONS S
AANLOOP ST
DIAMANT ST
BUITEKANT ST

Copyright © Map Studio MMI

Freeway
National Route
Main Through Route
Other Road
Route Markers
Built-up A
Park

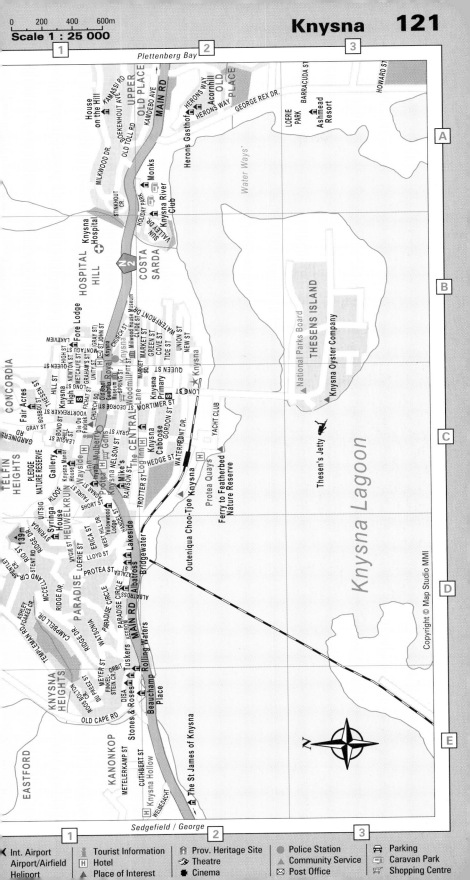

Scale 1 : 25 000

0 200 400 600m

Plettenberg Bay

Sedgefield / George

Copyright © Map Studio MMI

Key features/labels visible on map:

House on the Hill · UPPER OLD PLACE · OLD PLACE · Herons Gasthof · Herons Way · Aconhill · George Rex Dr. · LOERIE PARK · Ashmead Resort · BARRACUDA ST · HOWARD ST · Monks · Water Ways · Knysna River Club · HOSPITAL HILL · Knysna Hospital · COSTA SARDA · National Parks Board · THESENS ISLAND · Knysna Oyster Company · Fore Lodge · Milwood House Museum · CONCORDIA · Fair Acres · The CENTRAL · Knysna High · Royal Knysna · Die ou Pastorie · Old Gaol Museum · Knysna Caboose · Knysna Primary · Queen St · Union St · New St · YACHT CLUB · Thesen's Jetty · TELFIN HEIGHTS · PLEDGE NATURE RESERVE · Syringa House · Gallery · Wayside · Mike's · Protea Hotel · Knysna Manor House · Yellowwood Lodge · The Mulberry · Log Inn · HEUWELKRUIN · PARADISE · RIO 139m · Lakeside · Bridgewater · Albatross · Outeniqua Choo-Tjoe Knysna · Protea Quays · Ferry to Featherbed Nature Reserve · Knysna Lagoon · Rolling Waters · Stones & Roses · Tuskers · Beauchamp Place · KNYSNA HEIGHTS · OLD CAPE RD · The St James of Knysna · KANONKOP · Knysna Hollow · EASTFORD

Legend:

- ⟨ Int. Airport
- Airport/Airfield
- Heliport
- ℹ Tourist Information
- Ⓗ Hotel
- ▲ Place of Interest
- Prov. Heritage Site
- Theatre
- Cinema
- Police Station
- Community Service
- ✉ Post Office
- Parking
- Caravan Park
- Shopping Centre

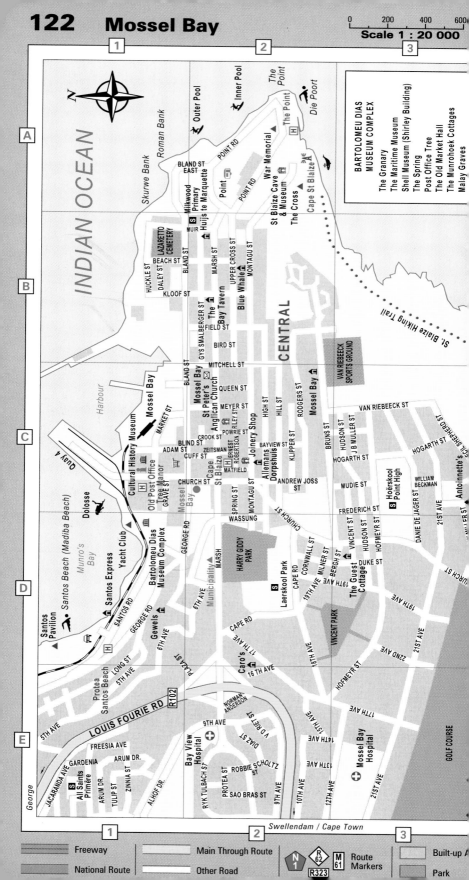

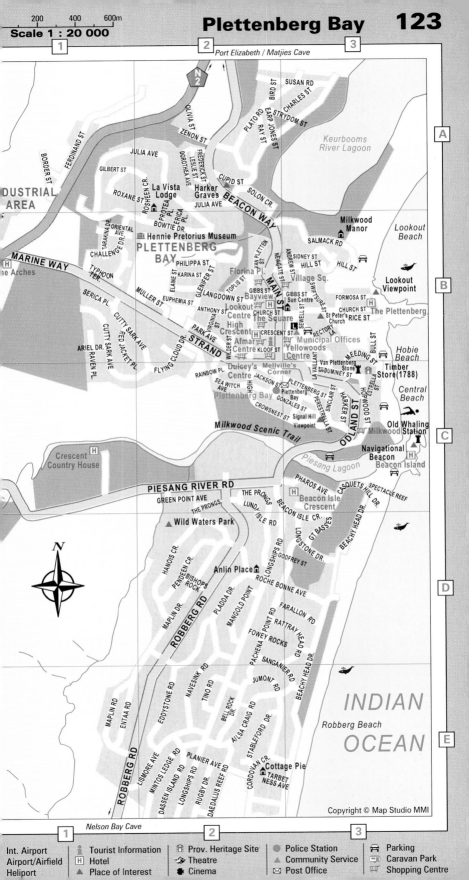

TOURIST REGION - CAPE METROPOLITAN AREA
V & A WATERFRONT

NAME	PG	GRID	NAME	PG	GRID	NAME	PG	GRID	NAME

General Information

Alfred Mall Shopping Centre	37	B 2	Kings Warehouse Shopping Centre	37	B 1	Somerset Hospital	37	C 1	Visitors Publicity Centre
			Red Shed Craft Warehouse Shopping Centre	37	B 1	Victoria Wharf Shopping Centre	37	B 1		Waterfront Post Office

TOURIST REGION - CAPE METROPOLITAN AREA
CAPE TOWN

NAME	PG	GRID	NAME	PG	GRID	NAME	PG	GRID	NAME

Streets

NAME	PG	GRID	NAME	PG	GRID	NAME	PG	GRID	NAME
Aandblom St.	39	E 4	Brook St.	39	D 6	Dawes St.	38	C 3	Grey St.
Adderley St.	39	C 4	Brownlow Rd.	38	D 2	De Hoop Ave.	38	E 1	Grey's Pass
Adelaide Rd.	39	E 6	Brunswick Rd.	38	D 2	De Korte Ave.	39	E 4	Grimsby Rd.
Albert Rd.	38	D 1	Bryant St.	38	D 2	De Lorentz St.	38	E 2	Grove Rd.
Albertus St.	39	D 4	Buiten St.	38	D 2	De Roos St.	39	D 4	Gympie St.
Aldgate St.	39	D 6	Buitengracht St.	38	D 3	De Villiers St.	39	E 4	Hall St.
Alexander St.	39	D 6	Buitenkant St.	38	E 3	De Waal Dr.	39	E 4	Hanover
Alexandra Pl.	38	A 1	Buitensingle St.	38	D 2	Dean St.	38	D 3	Hans Strijdom Ave.
Alfred St.	38	C 3	Bureau St.	38	D 3	Delft La.	38	D 3	Harrington St.
Alfred St.	39	B 4	Burg St.	38	C 3	Delphinium St.	39	E 4	Hastings St.
Alkmaar Rd.	39	C 6	Burnside Rd.	38	D 1	Derry	39	E 4	Hatfield Rd.
Anemone Ave.	39	E 4	Byron St.	38	E 1	Derwent Rd.	38	E 2	Hatfield St.
Annandale Rd.	38	E 3	Caleb St.	39	E 6	Devonport Rd.	38	D 1	Hay Rd.
Antrim Rd.	38	B 1	Caledon St.	39	D 4	Dillon La.	39	D 6	Haytor Rd.
Armadale St.	39	D 6	Camberwell Rd.	38	B 1	Dixon St.	38	C 3	Heere St.
Arum St.	39	E 4	Cambridge Ave.	38	E 1	Dock Rd.	39	B 4	Heerengracht
Ashstead Rd.	38	B 2	Cambridge St.	39	E 6	Dolls House	38	A 1	Helliger La.
Aspeling St.	39	E 5	Camden St.	38	E 1	Dorman St.	38	D 2	Hercules St.
Assurance La.	38	C 3	Camp St.	38	E 2	Dormehl La.	39	D 5	Hertzog Blvd.
Astana St.	38	C 2	Canterbury St.	39	D 4	Dormehl St.	39	D 5	Hiddengh Ave.
August St.	38	C 2	Cardiff St.	38	B 3	Dorp La.	38	C 3	High St.
Avenue Rd.	38	E 3	Carisbrook St.	38	D 2	Dorp St.	38	D 3	Highfield Rd.
Avondale Rd.	38	B 1	Carl St.	38	C 2	Dorset St.	39	D 5	Highfield St.
Bantam St.	38	C 2	Carreg Cr.	38	B 2	Douglas Pl.	39	D 6	Highfield Ter.
Barnabas St.	38	E 2	Carstens St.	38	D 2	Draklow St.	39	D 6	Hildene Rd.
Barnet St.	38	E 3	Castle St.	38	C 3	Drury La.	39	E 4	Hill
Barnham Ave.	39	E 4	Cauvin St.	39	E 5	Duke St.	39	E 6	Hill Rd.
Barrack St.	38	D 3	Cavalcade Rd.	38	B 2	Duncan Rd.	39	B 4	Hillside Rd.
Barron St.	39	D 6	Caxton St.	39	D 6	Dunkley St.	38	E 3	Hillside Ter.
Bartholomeu Dias	39	C 4	Chapel La., off Sidney St.	39	D 5	Dysart Rd.	38	B 2	Hof St.
Basket La.	39	E 5	Chapel St.	39	D 5	East Pier Rd.	39	A 4	Hofmeyer La.
Bath St., off Derwent	38	E 1	Chelsea Ave.	39	E 4	Eastern Blvd.	39	D 5	Hofmeyr St.
Battery Cr.	38	B 1	Chepstow Rd.	38	B 2	Eaton Rd.	38	E 2	Hope La.
Battery St.	38	B 3	Chester Rd.	39	E 6	Ebenezer St.	38	B 3	Hope St.
Bay Rd.	38	A 1	Cheviot Pl.	38	B 2	Ella St.	38	C 2	Hopeville St.
Bay View Ave.	38	E 1	Chiappini St.	38	C 3	Erica St.	39	E 6	Hospital St.
Beach Rd.	38	A 1	Christiaan St.	39	E 5	Exhibition Ter.	38	B 2	Hout La.
Beach Rd.	38	A 2	Church Sq., off Parliament St.	38	C 3	Faure St.	38	E 2	Hout St.
Beaumont	38	B 3	Church St.	38	D 3	Fawley Ter.	39	E 4	Hudson St.
Beckham St.	38	D 2	Civic Ave.	39	C 4	Firdale Rd.	38	E 1	Hyde St.
Bedford St.	38	E 3	Clare St.	38	C 2	Fish La.	38	C 3	Ilkley Cr.
Belle Ombre Rd.	38	D 1	Clive St.	39	E 4	Fish Quay Rd.	38	B 3	Invery Pl.
Belmont La.	38	E 3	Clovelly Ave.	39	E 4	Foregate St.	39	D 6	Ivanhoe St.
Ben Nevis Rd.	38	B 2	Clyde Rd.	38	B 1	Forest Hill Ave.	38	E 3	Ivy St.
Bennett St.	38	B 3	Clydebank Rd.	38	B 1	Fort Wynyard Rd.	38	A 3	Ixia Ave.
Bennington Rd.	38	D 2	Cobern St.	38	B 3	Francis St.	39	D 5	Jack Craig St.
Berg La.	38	C 3	Coen Steytler Ave.	39	C 4	Frederick Cl.	38	D 1	Jackson La.
Berrio Rd.	39	C 6	Commercial St.	38	D 3	Frederick St.	38	C 2	Jamieson St.
Bertrand Rd.	38	B 2	Constitution	39	E 5	Freeman	38	B 2	Jan Smuts St.
Beyers Rd.	39	D 6	Coodes Cr.	39	B 4	Frere St.	39	D 6	Jarvis St.
Bill Peters Dr.	38	A 1	Cornwall St.	39	D 6	Fritz Sonnenberg Rd.	38	A 2	Jasper St.
Blinde St.	39	E 5	Coronation Ave.	38	E 2	Gallery La.	38	D 3	Jersey St.
Bloem St.	38	D 3	Coronation Rd.	39	E 6	Gallows Hill Rd.	38	B 3	Jetty La.
Bloemhof St.	39	D 4	Corporation St.	38	D 3	Gardenia Ave.	39	E 4	Jetty St.
Bond St.	38	E 1	Cotswold Ave.	38	E 1	Gilmour Hills Rd.	38	D 1	Jordaan St.
Boundary Rd.	38	B 3	Courville	38	E 3	Glengariff Ter., off St. Bede's Rd.	38	B 1	Joubert Rd.
Bouquet St.	38	D 3	Coventry Rd.	39	E 6	Glynn St.	38	E 3	Justisie St.
Bowlers Way	38	A 1	Crassula Ave.	39	E 4	Glynnville Ter.	38	E 3	Keerom St.
Braemar St.	38	B 2	Croxteth Rd.	38	B 2	Gordon St.	38	E 3	Keizersgracht
Braeside	38	B 2	Cullinan	39	C 4	Gore St.	39	D 4	Kelvin Rd.
Brandweer St.	39	E 4	Curtis Rd.	38	E 2	Government Ave.	38	E 2	Kelvin St.
Breakwater	38	A 3	Cyprus St.	39	D 6	Grand Vue Rd.	39	E 6	Kenmore Rd.
Breda St.	38	E 3	D.F. Malan St.	39	C 4	Granger Bay	38	A 3	Kent Ave.
Bree St.	38	D 3	Darling St.	39	D 4	Granger St.	38	A 3	Kent La., off Vernon Terras Cr.
Bridge St.	39	E 6	Darter's Rd.	38	D 2	Gray St.	39	D 5	Keppel St.
			Davidson St.	39	D 6	Green	39	E 6	Kerchoff La., off Hope St.
						Green St.	38	D 3	

NAME	PG	GRID
St., off		
er Rd.	38	B 3
a.	38	A 1
	38	D 2
	39	E 6
	39	D 5
	38	E 2
Rd.	38	E 2
	38	E 2
	38	E 2
t.	38	D 2
off		
iff Rd.	38	B 1
	38	E 2
	39	D 5
St.	38	E 2
t.	39	E 4
	38	B 1
	38	D 1
St.	38	E 1
	38	D 3
dal Cr.	38	E 1
voet Rd.	38	D 2
Gr., off		
d.	38	B 1
Rd., off		
mbre Rd.	38	E 1
	38	D 3
t.	39	D 6
	39	E 6
	39	D 5
	38	B 3
	38	E 2
t.	38	D 2
Ter., off		
d Rd.	38	B 2
d.	38	B 3
	38	E 3
	38	D 3
ket St.	38	C 2
ket St.	38	D 3
	38	D 3
adner St.	39	C 5
urg St.	39	C 4
ein St.	39	D 4
	39	E 4
n Cl.	39	E 4
	38	B 1
	38	A 1
	38	E 2
d., off		
orge's Rd.	38	B 1
ve.	38	E 2
St., off Long St.	38	D 3
Rd.	39	E 6
erschlag Way	39	C 5
St., off		
vry Rd.	39	D 4
St., off		
d Rd.	38	B 1
La., off		
ercial St.	38	D 3
St.	38	E 3
e St.	39	E 4
St.	38	C 3
anean	39	C 5
ne Rd.	39	E 6
n Rd.	38	B 2
	38	D 2
	39	E 6
Steps	38	D 2
Rd.	38	E 2
	38	E 3
Steps	38	D 2
St.	39	D 6
d.	38	D 2
g La.	39	D 5
Rd.	38	E 2
e St.	39	D 6
	38	E 3

NAME	PG	GRID
Moreland Ter.	38	B 3
Morkel	38	E 2
Morkel St.	38	D 2
Morris La., off Signal	38	D 2
Mostert St.	39	D 4
Mount Rd.	39	D 4
Muir St.	39	D 5
Munnik La., off		
Keizersgracht	39	E 5
Myrtle St.	38	E 3
Nairn St.	39	D 6
Napier St.	38	C 3
Nelson St.	39	D 5
New Church	38	D 2
New Church St.	38	D 3
New Market St.	39	D 5
Newport St.	38	E 1
Nicol St.	38	E 2
Norfolk St.	39	D 6
Ocean	39	C 6
Ocean View Dr.	38	B 1
Oester La., off		
Vernon Terras Cr.	39	E 4
Old Marine Dr.	39	C 4
Orange St.	38	D 2
Orphan La.	38	D 2
Osborne St.	39	D 5
Oswald Pirow St.	39	D 4
Paddock	38	D 3
Page La.	39	D 6
Page St.	39	D 6
Parade St.	39	D 4
Park House Rd.	38	D 2
Park Rd.	38	A 1
Park Rd.	38	D 2
Park Rd.	39	E 6
Parliament La.	38	D 3
Peace St., off		
Carisbrook St.	38	D 2
Peak Rd.	39	E 4
Penarth Rd.	38	B 1
Pentz Rd.	38	C 2
Pepper St.	38	D 3
Percy St., off Hope St.	38	E 3
Perth Rd.	39	E 4
Perth St.	39	E 5
Philips	39	D 5
Pine Rd.	38	B 2
Pine Rd.	39	D 6
Plantation Rd.	38	C 2
Plein St.	39	D 4
Plum La., off		
Sir Lowry Rd.	39	D 6
Pontac La., off Kuyper St.	39	E 4
Pontac St.	39	E 6
Port Rd.	38	B 3
Portswood Rd.	38	B 2
Poyser Rd.	38	D 2
Premier St.	39	D 6
Prestwich St.	38	B 3
Primrose	39	D 4
Princess St.	39	E 6
Pypies Sq.	39	E 4
Quarry Hill Rd.	38	E 1
Queen	39	D 5
Queen Victoria St.	38	D 1
Queens Rd.	38	D 1
Queens Rd.	39	E 6
Rael St.	38	E 1
Ravenscraig Rd.	38	B 1
Ravenscraig Rd.	39	E 6
Rawbone La., off		
Rawbone St.	38	B 3
Rawbone St.	38	B 3
Reform St.	39	D 5
Regent St.	38	E 1
Reumee St.	38	D 2
Rheede St.	38	D 2
Richmond Rd.	38	A 1
Riebeek La., off		
Riebeek St.	38	C 3

NAME	PG	GRID
Riebeek St.	38	C 3
Roeland La.	39	E 4
Roeland St.	38	E 3
Roger St.	39	D 5
Roggebaai Sq.	39	C 4
Romney Rd.	38	B 1
Roodehek St.	38	E 3
Roodehek Ter.	38	E 3
Roos Rd.	38	B 2
Rose St.	38	C 3
Rothesay Pl.	38	A 1
Rua Bartolemeu Dias	39	C 4
Rua Vasco Da Gama	39	C 4
Russell St.	39	D 5
Sachs	38	D 2
Saddle Rd.	38	E 4
Salazar Sq.	39	C 4
Salmon St.	39	E 6
Schiere St., off		
Napier St.	38	C 3
Scholtz St.	38	B 1
Schoonder St.	38	E 3
Scott St.	38	E 3
Sea St., off		
Waterkant St.	38	C 3
Searle St.	39	D 6
Selkirk St.	39	D 5
Selwyn St.	39	D 6
Selwyn Ter.	39	D 6
Sheppard La., off		
Kuyper St.	39	E 4
Sheppard St.	39	E 5
Shortmarket St.	38	C 3
Sidney St., off Tennant	39	D 4
Signal Hill Rd.	38	C 1
Signal St.	38	C 3
Sir Lowry Rd.	39	D 4
Skyway	38	B 2
Smart La., off Wicht Cr.	39	D 4
Solan St.	39	E 4
Sollum St.	38	B 1
Somerset Rd.	38	B 3
Sorey La., off		
Caledon St.	39	D 4
South Arm Rd.	39	A 4
Southgate St.	39	D 6
Spin St.	38	D 3
Springbok Rd.	38	B 1
Springfield Ter.	39	E 5
St. Bede's Rd.	38	B 1
St. George's Mall	39	C 4
St. George's Rd.	38	B 1
St. John's St.	38	D 3
St. Marks St.	39	E 5
St. Martin's Rd., off		
St. Bede's Rd.	38	B 1
St. Mary's La.	38	D 3
St. Michael's Rd.	38	E 1
St. Quintons Rd.	38	E 3
Stadzicht St.	38	C 2
Stal Sq.	38	D 3
Stanley Pl.	38	A 1
Station Rd.	39	D 6
Stephan Way	38	A 1
Stephen St.	38	E 2
Steyning St.	39	E 6
Strand St.	39	D 4
Stuckeris St.	39	D 5
Sussex St.	39	D 6
Sydney St.	38	B 2
Tamboerskloof Rd.	38	D 2
Tanabaru St.	38	C 2
Teck	39	E 6
Tennant St.	39	D 4
Thornhill Rd.	38	B 2
Three Anchor Bay Rd.	38	A 3
Torbay Rd.	38	B 3
Trafalgar Pl.	39	D 4
Trent Rd.	38	E 1
Tuin Sq., off Vrede St.	38	E 3
Tuin St.	38	E 2

NAME	PG	GRID
Tulbagh Sq., off		
Hans Strijdom Ave.	39	C 4
Turnbull	38	E 3
Ummah Cl.	39	D 5
Union St.	38	E 2
University St., off		
Victoria St.	38	D 2
Upper	38	E 2
Upper Adelaide	39	E 6
Upper Albert Rd.	38	E 1
Upper Bloem St.	38	C 2
Upper Buitengracht St.	38	D 2
Upper Cambridge St.	39	E 6
Upper Canterbury St.	39	E 4
Upper Coventry Rd.	39	E 6
Upper Duke St.	39	E 6
Upper Hillside Ter.	38	B 3
Upper Leeuwen St.	38	C 2
Upper Maynard St.	38	E 3
Upper Mill St.	39	E 4
Upper Pepper St.	38	C 2
Upper Portswood Rd.	38	B 2
Upper Queens Rd.	39	E 6
Upper Ravenscraig Rd.	39	E 6
Upper Union St.	38	E 2
Upper Warwick St.	39	E 6
Van der Leur Cl., off		
Vernon Terras Cr.	39	E 4
Van Ryneveld Ave.	39	C 6
Vanguard	39	C 6
Varney's Rd.	38	B 2
Varsity St.	38	E 1
Vasco da Gama Blvd.	39	C 4
Vernon Terras Cr.	39	E 4
Vesperdene Rd.	38	B 2
Victoria St.	38	E 2
Vine St.	38	E 2
Virginia Ave.	38	E 3
Vlei Rd.	38	A 2
Voetboog Rd.	38	C 2
Vogelgezang St.	39	E 5
Vos St.	38	E 3
Vrede St.	38	E 3
Vriende St.	38	C 3
Wale St.	38	C 3
Walmer Rd.	39	D 6
Walter Rd.	38	B 1
Wandel St.	38	E 2
Wandel St.	38	E 3
Warren St.	38	D 1
Warwick St.	39	E 6
Warwick St.	39	E 4
Waterkant St.	38	B 3
Waterkant St.	38	C 3
Watson St.	38	D 2
Watsonia St.	38	E 4
Welgemeend St.	38	E 2
Weltevreden St.	38	E 2
Wembley St.	38	E 3
Werf La., off		
Caledon St.	39	D 4
Wesley St.	38	B 2
Wessels	38	B 2
West	38	B 3
West Quay Rd.	38	B 3
West St., off		
Prestwich St.	38	C 3
Western Blvd.	38	A 2
Wharf St.	39	C 4
Whitford	38	D 2
Wicht Cr.	39	D 4
Wigtown Rd.	38	B 2
Wilkinson St.	38	E 2
William St.	39	D 6
Windburg Ave.	39	E 4
Woodlands Rd.	39	D 6
Woodside Rd.	38	D 1
Worcester St.	39	E 6
Wright St.	39	D 6
York Rd.	38	B 2
Yusuf Dr.	38	C 2

128

NAME	PG	GRID

General Information

NAME	PG	GRID
Cape Col High School	39	D 4
Cape Technicon	39	E 4
Cape Town High School	38	D 3
Cape Town Police Station	39	D 4
Cape Town Post Office	39	D 4
Chapelstraat Primary School	39	D 6
City Park Hospital	38	C 3
Conradie Recreation Ground	38	E 1
De Waal Park	38	E 2
Deutsche Schule zu Cape Town High School	38	D 1
Ellerton Primary School	38	B 1
Gardens Shopping Centre	38	E 3
Golden Acre Shopping Centre	39	D 4
Good Hope Shopping Centre	39	D 4
Good Hope Seminary Jnr. Primary School	38	E 3
Green Point & Sea Point Bowling Club	38	A 1
Green Point Post Office	38	B 2
Green Point Stadium	38	A 2
Green Point Track	38	A 2
Harold Cressey High School	39	E 2
Holy Cross Primary School	39	E 6
Jan van Riebeeck High School	38	E 2
Jan van Riebeeck Primary School	38	E 2
Kings Warehouse Shopping Centre	38	A 3
Kloof St. Post Office	38	E 2
Mariners College	39	B 4
Metropolitan Golf Course	38	A 2
Mill Street Post Office	38	E 3
Ramaniyeh Primary School	39	E 5
Roggebaai Post Office	39	C 4
Royal Cape Yacht Club	39	C 6
Sea Point High School	38	B 1
Sea Point Police Station	38	A 1
Somerset Hospital	38	A 3
St. Mary's Primary School		
St. Mary's Maternity Hospital		
Stal Plein Post Office		
Table Bay Harbour Police Station		
Tamboerskloof Primary School		
Three Anchor Bay Tennis Club		
UCT Business School		
Victoria Wharf Shopping Centre		
Vlaeberg Post Office		
Walmer Estate Prep Primary School		
Waterfront Post Office		
Woodstock Post Office		
Zonnebloem College		

NAME	PG	GRID

Streets

NAME	PG	GRID
A.F. Keen Dr.	40	C 2
Amanda Rd.	40	E 2
Apostle Steps, off Victoria Rd.	40	A 2
Arcadia Steps, off Victoria Rd	40	C 2
Argyle St.	40	C 2
Athol Rd.	40	B 3
Athol Rd. South	40	C 3
Barbara Rd.	40	E 2
Berkley Rd.	40	C 2
Beta	40	D 1
Biskop Steps	40	A 2
Blair Rd.	40	B 3
Blinkwater Rd.	40	D 2
Cairn Steps	40	A 2
Camps Bay	40	D 2
Camps Bay Dr.	40	C 3
Central Dr.	40	C 2
Chas Booth Ave.	40	E 2
Chilworth Rd.	40	B 2
Cliff Rd.	40	B 1
Clifton Rd.	40	B 2
Clifton Steps	40	B 2
Cohen Pl.	40	E 2
Comrie Rd.	40	C 3
Cramond Rd.	40	C 3
Cranberry Cr.	40	C 3
Crown Cr.	40	C 2
Dal Rd.	40	B 3
Dunkeld Rd.	40	D 2
Eldon La.	40	C 3
Farquhar	40	C 2
Fillians	40	C 2
Finchley Rd.	40	D 2
First Cr.	40	C 2
Fiskaal Cl.	40	D 2
Fiskaal Rd.	40	D 2
Francolin Rd.	40	D 3
Fulham Rd.	40	E 2
Geneva Dr.	40	C 3
Hely Hutchinson Ave.	40	C 2
Hoopoe La.	40	E 2
Horak Ave.	40	D 3
Houghton Rd.	40	D 2
Houghton Steps	40	D 2
Hove Rd.	40	D 2
Ingleside Rd.	40	D 2
Isadore Cohen Pl.	40	E 2
Kasteel Steps	40	A 2
Kinnoull Rd.	40	D 2
Kreef La.	40	D 1
Lincoln Rd.	40	C 2
Link St.	40	D 2
Lower Kloof Rd.	40	B 2
Medburn Rd.	40	C 3
Montana Rd.	40	C 3
Mount Pleasant Steps	40	A 2
Nettleton Rd.	40	A 2
Ottawa Ave.	40	E 2
Oudekraal Rd.	40	E 2
Park Rd.	40	E 2
Penelope Cl.	40	E 2
Petrel Cl.	40	E 2
Pitlochry Rd.	40	E 1
Platteklip Sq.	40	D 3
Prima Ave.	40	C 3
Quebec St.	40	C 2
Ravensteyn Rd.	40	D 3
Ronald Ave.	40	C 2
Rontree Ave.	40	E 2
Roslyn La.	40	D 2
Rottingdean Rd.	40	D 2
Round House Rd.	40	B 2
Sedgemoor Rd.	40	C 2
Shanklin Cr.	40	B 3
Stern Cl.	40	E 1
Strathearn Ave.	40	D 2
Strathmore La., off Strathmore Rd.	40	C 2
Strathmore Rd.	40	C 2
Susan Ave.	40	E 2
Sybil La.	40	C 2
Terminus Steps	40	E 1
The Cheviots		
The Drive		
The Fairway		
The Grange Rd.		
The Meadows		
The Meadway		
The Ridge		
Theresa Ave.		
Totness Ave.		
Twenty Steps		
Upper Tree Rd.		
Van Kampz St.		
Victoria Rd.		
Willesden Rd.		
Woodford Rd.		
Woodhead Cl.		

General Informat...

NAME	PG	GRID
Camps Bay Police Station		
Camps Bay Post Office		
Camps Bay Prep		
Camps Bay Primary		
Camps Bay Secondary School		
Glen Country Club		

NAME	PG	GRID

Streets

NAME	PG	GRID
Abington Cir.	41	C 3
Addo Rd.	41	C 3
Amsterdam Ave.	41	B 1
Ballycline Steps	41	D 2
Banks Rd.	41	C 3
Bato Rd.	41	E 2
Beach Rd.	41	C 2
Bee Eater	41	B 2
Belvedere Ave.	41	B 3
Berg Rd.	41	C 1
Bethel Rd.	41	A 2
Brand St.	41	E 2
Brunswick St.	41	E 2
Brussels Ave.	41	B 1
Burton La.	41	D 2
Camilla St.	41	E 2
Carlton Rd.	41	B 2
Central Cir.	41	C 2
Central Rd.	41	C 2
Clan Stewart St.	41	E 2
Cliff Rd.	41	D 3
Clovelly Rd.	41	B 3
Clovelly Steps	41	A 3
Cobern La.	41	C 1
Cockburn Cl.	41	E 2
Cockburn St.	41	E 2
Cockle Cr.	41	B 2
Columbus Ave.	41	B 1
Contour Way	41	D 2
Cronwright La.	41	C 1
Dalton Rd.	41	C 2
Darlington	41	B 1
De Villiers Steps	41	D 2
De Waal Rd.	41	C 2
De Waal Rd. Upper	41	C 1
Delford Ave.	41	B 2
Disa Ave.	41	B 2
Drongo	41	B 2
Dunster Ave.	41	C 2
Echo Rd.	41	D 3
Echo Steps	41	D 3
Eighth Ave.	41	C 2
Eleventh Ave.	41	C 1
Elgin Cir.	41	B 2
Emerald Cr.	41	B 2
Exeter Ave.	41	B 2
Fairbairn St.	41	E 2
Fife Ave.	41	B 1
Fifteenth Ave.		
Fifth Ave.		
First Ave.		
First Cr.		
Fourteenth Ave.		
Fourth Ave.		
Genoa Ave.		
Glindon Rd.		
Golconda St.		
Greenhill Cl.		
Grysbok Way		
Highway		
Hillside Rd.		
Hilton Rd.		
Hobbs Steps		
Ivanhoe St.		
Jasmine Ave.		

TOURIST REGION - CAPE METROPOLITAN AREA
FISH HOEK
CONT.

NAME	PG	GRID	NAME	PG	GRID	NAME	PG	GRID
Rd.	41	B 1	Orlando Rd.	41	C 1	Seventeenth Ave.	41	C 1	
Cr.	41	C 1	Outspan Steps	41	D 2	Seventh	41	C 1	
y Rd.	41	B 1	Palm	41	B 1	Seventh Ave.	41	C 2	
Rd.	41	B 1	Paris	41	C 1	Simonstown Rd.	41	D 3	
n Rd.	41	B 1	Peak Rd.	41	D 1	Sixteenth Ave.	41	C 1	
Rd.	41	B 1	Peers Hill	41	B 1	Sixth Ave.	41	C 2	
dare Cr.	41	C 1	Peri Rd.	41	B 2	Springbok Way	41	C 2	
nrae Cr.	41	C 1	Pinoak Cr.	41	B 1	Steenbok Way	41	C 2	
	41	B 2	Prinia	41	B 2	Sunnycove Steps	41	D 3	
	41	D 2	Pritchard Steps	41	D 2	Sunray Rd.	41	B 1	
	41	E 3	Promenade Rd.	41	B 3	Syringa Cl.	41	B 1	
Steps	41	A 2	Protea Ave.	41	C 2	Tenth Ave.	41	C 1	
	41	B 3	Ranger	41	C 1	The Close	41	B 2	
Rd.	41	B 1	Ravine Steps	41	D 2	Third Ave.	41	C 2	
e Ave.	41	A 2	Recreation Rd.	41	C 2	Third Cr.	41	C 1	
Steps	41	D 3	Retief La.	41	C 2	Thirteenth Ave.	41	C 1	
n Rd.	41	B 3	Ribbok Way	41	C 2	Twelfth Ave.	41	C 1	
n Rd.	41	D 2	Rice La.	41	C 2	Upper Kildare Cr.	41	C 1	
	41	C 1	Rickard La.	41	C 1	Upper Kinrae Cr.	41	C 2	
ve.	41	C 2	Roseberry Ave.	41	B 3	Upper			
r.	41	B 2	Ross La.	41	C 1	Recreation Rd.	41	C 1	
ve.	41	C 1	Saunders Cl.	41	B 1	Winkle Way	41	B 2	
lk	41	B 2	Second Ave.	41	D 2	Yselstein St.	41	E 2	
	41	B 2	Second Cr.	41	C 2	Zoutendyk Steps	41	D 2	

General Information

	PG	GRID
Bay (Jnr. Campus)	41	B 2
Clovelly Country Club	41	A 2
Fish Hoek Middle		
Secondary School	41	B 1
Fish Hoek		
Police Station	41	C 3
Fish Hoek		
Primary School	41	C 1
Fish Hoek Snr School	41	C 1
Paul Greyling		
Primary School	41	C 2
Shoprite		
Shopping Centre	41	C 3
The Arcade		
Shopping Centre	41	C 2
Town Square		
Shopping Centre	41	C 2
Valyland Post Office	41	B 1
Valyland		
Shopping Centre	41	C 1
Vishoek Post Office	41	C 2

TOURIST REGION - CAPE METROPOLITAN AREA
HOUT BAY

Streets

NAME	PG	GRID	NAME	PG	GRID	NAME	PG	GRID
			Empire Ave.	42	D 2	Nerine St.	42	D 3	The Promenade	42	E 2
ak St.	42	B 2	Erica St.	42	D 3	Nooitgedacht Rd.	42	B 1	Union St.	42	D 3
d.	42	C 1	Gibraltar	42	E 1	Norman Rd.	42	C 1	Ursina Cl.	42	C 1
er Ave.	42	D 2	Gilquin Cr.	42	D 1	North Shore Dr.	42	E 1	Valley Rd.	42	B 2
er Ave.	42	D 2	Gordon Rd.	42	C 1	O.R. Tambo Rd.	42	B 3	Valley Rd.	42	B 2
Cl.	42	A 2	Governor's Wk.	42	B 1	Orange St.	42	D 3	Valley View	42	A 1
s Rd.	42	D 3	H. Peterson Ave.	42	B 3	Orbea Cl.	42	C 1	Van Hoogstraten Rd.	42	C 3
Rd.	42	C 2	Harbour Lights	42	D 1	Oxford St.	42	D 1	Van Oudtshoorn Rd.	42	B 2
nevere	42	D 3	Helgarda Ave.	42	B 1	Park Ave.	42	A 2	Victor St.	42	C 1
d.	42	C 2	Henschell Rd.	42	C 1	Payne Rd.	42	C 2	Victoria	42	D 1
s Cl.	42	E 3	Honeysuckle Cl.	42	D 3	Penzance Ave.	42	C 2	Victoria Ave	42	C 1
skloof Rd.	42	E 3	Hughenden Rd.	42	B 3	Perrault Rd.	42	C 1	Victoria Rd.	42	C 2
r.	42	E 3	Ixia St.	42	D 3	Pinedene Rd.	42	D 3	Victorskloof Rd.	42	A 2
ath	42	D 3	Johan St.	42	D 3	Plumtree Ave.	42	B 3	Vineyard Way	42	C 2
Rd.	42	A 3	Karakal Rd.	42	B 1	Pondicherry Ave.	42	C 1	Welbevind Way	42	A 3
p Rd.	42	B 1	King Rd.	42	E 3	Princess St.	42	D 2	Westerford	42	B 2
e-Noir Cl.	42	C 2	Lair Ave.	42	B 1	Printzia Cl.	42	C 1	Westford Rd.	42	E 1
n St.	42	D 2	Lancaster St.	42	C 1	Promenade Rd.	42	E 2	Willow Way	42	B 1
d.	42	C 2	Lategan Rd.	42	C 2	R. Sobukwe St.	42	B 3	Wood Rd.	42	D 2
ll St.	42	D 3	Laurentia Way	42	C 1	Riverside Ter.	42	A 3	Woodcutters Cl.	42	B 3
	42	D 1	Leeuloop	42	B 1	Rochea	42	C 1	Worcester St.	42	C 1
gne Cr.	42	D 2	Lentedal Rd.	42	B 1	Royal Ave.	42	D 1	Zoutman Cl.	42	D 1
nay La.	42	D 2	Linda	42	C 1	Royland Cr.	42	C 1			
Cr.	42	D 3	Lindevista	42	E 3	S. Biko St.	42	B 2			
an St.	42	C 3	Little Lions Head	42	A 1	Sagewood Dr.	42	D 3			
t.	42	D 1	Liverpool St.	42	D 1	Salisbury Rd.	42	E 1			
nion La.	42	B 1	Louw Rd.	42	C 2	Sandpiper Pl.	42	C 1			
	42	D 3	Luisa	42	A 2	Scott Rd.	42	D 3			
St.	42	C 1	Luisa Way	42	B 2	Scottsville Cir.	42	D 3			
St.	42	D 3	Main Rd.	42	C 2	Seacliffe Rd.	42	E 1			
	42	C 2	Manchester Rd.	42	C 1	Sheeda Rd.	42	B 1			
onnes Ave.	42	B 2	Marais Rd.	42	D 3	Shiraz Blvd.	42	D 2			
d.	42	B 1	Martingale Ave.	42	A 3	Silvertree	42	B 2			
	42	D 1	Melkhout Cr.	42	D 2	Skaife St.	42	D 3			
d.	42	B 1	Melkhout St.	42	E 2	Sluysken Rd.	42	E 1			
Rd.	42	D 1	Military	42	E 3	St. Anthonys Rd.	42	D 2			
ay	42	B 2	Milner Ave.	42	D 2	Stirrup La.	42	A 3			
			Mount Rhodes Dr.	42	A 1	Sunbush Cl.	42	C 3			
			Mountain St.	42	C 1	Surcingle Ave.	42	A 2			
			N.R. Mandela Rd.	42	B 3	Suther Cl.	42	A 1			

General Information

	PG	GRID
Dominican Grimley		
Special School	42	A 2
Hout Bay		
Police Station	42	E 2
Hout Bay Post Office	42	D 2
Hout Bay Yacht Club	42	E 1
Kronendal		
Primary School	42	D 3
Mainstream		
Shopping Centre	42	D 2
Melkhout		
Shopping Centre	42	D 2
Oranjekloof Moraviese		
Primary School	42	B 3

TOURIST REGION - CAPE METROPOLITAN AREA
MILNERTON

Streets

NAME	PG	GRID	NAME	PG	GRID	NAME	PG	GRID
s Cl.	43	B 3	Aerial Rd.	43	C 3	Algoa Rd.	43	D 1	Aquarius Rd.	43	B 3
			Alamein Rd.	43	B 1	Angas Rd.	43	D 2	Aries Rd.	43	B 3
			Albow Rd.	43	E 1	Apollo Way	43	B 3	Arum St.	43	B 2

TOURIST REGION - CAPE METROPOLITAN AREA
MILNERTON cont.

NAME	PG	GRID	NAME	PG	GRID	NAME	PG	GRID	NAME
Ascot Rd.	43	B 2	Freesia St.	43	B 2	Masson Rd.	43	C 2	School St.
Ashton Rd.	43	D 1	Fuchsia St.	43	C 3	Max Rd.	43	E 1	Shayele Rd.
Athena Way	43	A 3	Galton St.	43	D 2	Mbhongisa Ave.	43	B 3	Sheldon Rd.
Atlas Dr.	43	B 3	Gannet St.	43	E 2	Meadow Rd.	43	D 1	Shoal Creek Mews
Augusta Mews	43	A 1	Gardenia Way	43	A 2	Mercury Way	43	B 3	Sikhova Cr.
Bancroft Rd.	43	E 1	Gazala	43	B 1	Meurant Rd.	43	E 2	Skhwalimanzi Ct.
Barrow Rd.	43	C 2	Gemini Rd.	43	B 3	Milkway Dr.	43	B 3	Skyliner Ave.
Bay Beach Ave	43	A 1	Glanville St.	43	D 2	Millvale Rd.	43	C 1	Sparta Way
Beaufort Rd.	43	D 1	Gluckman Ave.	43	E 1	Mimosa Cr.	43	A 2	St. Andrews Mews
Begonia St.	43	B 2	Gousblom St.	43	D 2	Mimosa St.	43	A 2	St. Pierre St.
Benghazi	43	B 1	Graaff Ave.	43	A 2	Mitford Rd.	43	C 2	Tanglewood Cr.
Berkdale Mews	43	A 1	Greyton Rd.	43	D 1	Mqokotho Ave.	43	A 3	Taurus Rd.
Bhayi Ave.	43	B 3	Guia Rd.	43	C 3	Nahum St.	43	E 1	Theal St.
Bhofolo Ave.	43	B 3	Hawston Rd.	43	D 1	Namar Rd.	43	C 3	Tijgerhof
Bolmear St.	43	E 1	Heather St.	43	A 2	Nautilus Way	43	B 3	Triton Way
Bosmansdam Rd.	43	C 3	Helios Cir.	43	B 3	Nemesia Cr.	43	A 2	Troon Mews
Boundary Rd.	43	D 1	Helwan Rd.	43	B 1	Nemesia St.	43	A 2	Tulbagh Rd.
Breezand Rd.	43	C 2	Hem Dr.	43	B 3	Neptune Rd.	43	B 3	Umnquna Ct.
Bremer St.	43	D 1	Hercules Dr.	43	B 3	Nerina St.	43	A 3	Umtata Dr.
Bridge Rd.	43	C 1	Heron Bay Mews	43	A 1	Ngqabe Cr.	43	B 3	Umthathi Ave.
Broad Rd.	43	B 2	Hlungule Cr. East	43	B 3	Nieuhof	43	C 2	Umthuma Cr.
Burchell St.	43	D 2	Hobe Rd. North	43	B 3	Noble Rd.	43	C 2	Union Ave.
Burmeister Cir.	43	D 1	Houtman St.	43	D 2	Nomyayi Dr.	43	B 3	Union St.
Cala Cr.	43	B 3	Hussar St.	43	E 1	Norwood Rd.	43	C 1	Uno Rd.
Cancer Rd.	43	B 3	Ibex	43	D 2	Ntsikizi Ave.	43	B 3	Uplands Rd.
Capricorn Way	43	B 3	Icarus Way	43	B 3	Oakhill Mews	43	A 1	Vaal Rd.
Castle Pines Ter.	43	A 1	Imfene Ct.	43	B 3	Oceanus Way	43	B 3	Valentyn Rd.
Chandos Rd.	43	C 1	Impala Ave.	43	E 1	Oleander St.	43	A 3	Venus Ave.
Chepstowe St.	43	D 2	Indwe Rd.	43	D 1	Orange Rd.	43	D 1	Virgo St.
Coghill Mews	43	A 1	Iona St.	43	C 2	Orchard Rd.	43	C 2	Wayfarer Ave.
Coral Springs Mews	43	A 1	Isis Dr.	43	A 3	Orion Rd.	43	B 3	Weenen Rd.
Corsair Cl.	43	C 3	Ixia St.	43	A 2	Osirus Way	43	A 3	Weir Rd.
Corsair Rd.	43	C 3	Janssen St.	43	D 1	Oxalis	43	A 2	Westchester Mews
Cotswold Rd.	43	C 1	Janthina Cr.	43	B 3	Park Ave.	43	D 1	Westwind Rd.
Crassula St.	43	B 2	Jasmin St.	43	A 3	Park Ave.	43	D 1	Wilmot Rd.
Cumming Rd.	43	D 2	Jeppe Rd.	43	C 1	Pebble			Winton Cr.
Dada Dr.	43	B 3	Jupiter St.	43	A 3	Beach Mews	43	A 1	Xhalanga Ave.
Daisy Cir.	43	E 1	Kei Rd.	43	D 1	Peddie Rd.	43	C 2	Yarrow Rd.
Daniel Rd.	43	C 2	Kettle Way	43	E 1	Pegasus Rd.	43	B 3	Zalkin St.
Daniell	43	C 3	Keurboom St.	43	A 3	Pending Rd.	43	D 2	Zastron Rd.
Daniell Rd. East	43	C 3	Keurboom St.	43	C 3	Percival Rd.	43	C 2	Zeus Dr.
De Grendel Rd.	43	C 2	Kildare Rd.	43	C 1	Perseus Rd.	43	A 3	
Democracy Dr.	43	B 3	Kiln Rd.	43	D 1	Pienaar Rd.	43	A 2	General Information
Diana	43	C 3	Knysna Rd.	43	C 1	Pine St.	43	C 3	
Disa Cr.	43	C 3	Koeberg	43	D 1	Pisces Rd.	43	B 3	Canoe Club
Disa St.	43	B 2	Langerman Ave.	43	D 2	Pixie St.	43	E 1	Centre Point
Donegal St.	43	E 1	Latrobe Rd.	43	E 2	Pluto Cl.	43	B 3	Shopping Centre
Dordrecht Rd.	43	D 1	Layard	43	C 2	Port Bush Mews	43	A 1	De Grendel
Dreyer	43	E 1	Leo Rd.	43	B 3	Pringle Cl.	43	D 2	Spesiale Skool
Dune Rd.	43	D 1	Libra Cr.	43	B 3	Pringle Rd.	43	D 2	Milnerton
Dywabisini Ave.	43	A 3	Lincluden St.	43	E 1	Protea Cr.	43	E 1	Golf Course
Eclipse Rd.	43	C 3	Link Rd.	43	C 1	Protea St.	43	C 3	Milnerton Medi-Clinic
Elegance Rd.	43	C 3	Linnet St.	43	E 1	Quest Rd.	43	C 2	Milnerton
Elffers Rd.	43	E 2	Lobelia St.	43	A 3	Quigley Rd.	43	C 2	Police Station
Elgin Rd.	43	D 1	Lobelia St.	43	A 3	Qumba Cr.	43	B 3	Milnerton Post Office
Epping St.	43	E 1	Loxton Rd.	43	C 1	Ranisi Dr.	43	B 3	Milnerton
Erica St.	43	B 2	Lupin Cr.	43	A 2	Ratanga Rd.	43	C 3	Primary School
Eshowe Rd.	43	C 3	Madeira St.	43	E 1	Redlands Rd.	43	C 2	Milnerton
Esplanade	43	D 1	Magnolia Cr.	43	E 1	Reitz Rd.	43	D 2	Secondary School
Essam Rd.	43	B 1	Mansfield Mews	43	A 1	Rhemus St.	43	B 3	Milpark
Fairbridge Rd.	43	E 2	Mansveldt Rd.	43	C 2	Rider Haggard St.	43	D 2	Shopping Centre
Farnworth St.	43	E 1	Maple St.	43	C 3	Robin Rd.	43	C 1	Seamount
Firgrove Rd.	43	D 1	Marais Rd.	43	C 1	Romulus Rd.	43	B 3	Primary School
Fitzpatrick Rd.	43	C 2	Marehale Cr.	43	C 1	Sable Rd.	43	E 3	Tygerhof
Fitzpatrick Rd.	43	C 2	Marigold St.	43	A 3	Sable St.	43	D 1	Primary School
Forest Oaks Mews	43	A 1	Marloth Rd.	43	D 2	Sanctuary Cl.	43	C 1	Zonnekus
Freedom Way	43	B 3	Mars Way	43	B 3	Santos St.	43	E 1	Primary School
			Martel St.	43	D 2	Saturn Cir.	43	B 3	

TOURIST REGION - CAPE METROPOLITAN AREA
MUIZENBERG

NAME	PG	GRID	NAME	PG	GRID	NAME	PG	GRID	NAME
Streets			Approach St.	44	A 1	Barbourne Rd.	44	A 2	Bond St.
			Arthur Rd.	44	C 3	Bath Rd.	44	C 3	Boulder Rd.
			Atlantic Rd.	44	C 3	Battle Ridge	44	B 3	Boveney Rd.
			Auret Rd., off			Bay Rd.	44	D 2	Box Rd.
Admirals Wk.	44	B 3	Beach Rd.	44	D 2	Beach Rd.	44	D 2	Boyes
Albert Rd.	44	B 2	Axminster Rd.	44	C 3	Bedford Rd.	44	A 2	Braemar Rd.
Albertyn Rd.	44	C 2	Baker Rd.	44	C 3	Belvedere Rd.	44	C 2	Brandwood Rd.
Alexander Rd.	44	C 3							

TOURIST REGION - CAPE METROPOLITAN AREA
MUIZENBERG CONT.

NAME	PG	GRID	NAME	PG	GRID	NAME	PG	GRID	NAME	PG	GRID
Rd.	44	A 1	Fraser Rd.	44	C 3	Michel Rd.	44	A 3	St. Helier's Rd.	44	C 2
Rd.	44	C 3	Geneva Rd.	44	B 3	Milner Rd.	44	C 3	St. James Rd.	44	E 1
d Rd.	44	B 2	George St.	44	C 2	Mistral Cl.	44	A 1	Station Rd.	44	A 1
	44	B 2	Gerard Rd.	44	A 2	Moselle Rd.	44	E 1	Stellen Cl.	44	A 3
d.	44	A 1	Gill Rd.	44	C 2	Mount Rd.	44	C 2	Suffolk Rd.	44	A 1
end	44	A 3	Gloucester Rd.	44	A 1	Niblick St.	44	A 1	Talma Rd., off		
	44	A 3	Halyard Wk.	44	A 3	Norfolk Rd.	44	A 1	School Rd.	44	C 2
t.	44	A 1	Hansen Rd.	44	C 3	Northumberland Ave.	44	A 1	Thaxter Rd.	44	A 2
ge Rd.	44	A 2	Hants Rd.	44	C 2	Nottingham Rd.	44	A 1	The Row	44	B 3
l.	44	C 2	Harpenden Rd.	44	B 2	Old Boyes Dr.	44	B 2	Towers Rd.	44	C 2
sland Way	44	A 3	Hastings Rd.	44	B 3	Ombersley Rd.	44	A 2	Turks Head Cl.	44	A 3
hel Cl.	44	B 2	Henley Rd.	44	C 3	Orient Rd.	44	A 2	Uxbridge Rd.	44	A 2
.	44	E 1	Henwick Rd.	44	A 2	Palmer Rd.	44	C 3	Verwood St.	44	B 2
Cl.	44	A 3	Heytor Rd.	44	E 1	Park Island Way	44	A 3	Vlei Rd.	44	A 2
ok Rd.	44	D 2	Hillcrest Rd.	44	C 2	Park Rd.	44	C 2	Vlei Rd.	44	C 3
Rd.	44	A 2	Holland Rd.	44	C 3	Penrose Rd.	44	C 2	Walburg Rd.	44	B 2
d.	44	C 3	Iron St.	44	A 1	Pentrich Rd.	44	E 1	Watson Rd.	44	C 3
n Rd.	44	C 3	Jacobs Ladder	44	E 1	Promenade Rd.	44	A 2	Westbury Rd.	44	C 3
.	44	A 1	Karper Rd.	44	A 2	Recreation Rd.	44	C 3	Westray Rd.	44	E 1
n Rd.	44	C 3	Killarney Rd.	44	C 3	Rhodesia Rd.	44	C 2	Wherry Rd.	44	C 3
d.	44	B 3	Lea Rd.	44	A 2	Rodwell Rd.	44	E 1	Windermere Rd.	44	B 3
Rd.	44	B 2	Leicester Rd.	44	A 1	Ronleigh Rd.	44	C 2	Wynand Rd.	44	A 2
s Cl.	44	A 3	Leighton Rd.	44	E 1	Rooikrans Rd.	44	A 2	Yarmouth Rd.	44	B 3
l Rd.	44	A 1	Ley Rd.	44	E 1	Royal Rd.	44	C 3			
	44	A 2	Lincoln Fields Cr., off			Royston Rd.	44	A 2			
Rd.	44	B 2	Lincoln Rd.	44	A 1	Rusten Ct.	44	A 3	**General Information**		
Rd.	44	C 3	Lincoln Rd.	44	A 1	Rutter Rd.	44	A 1			
l.	44	A 3	Lynx Cl.	44	A 1	Sandhurst Rd.	44	E 1	Muizenberg Police		
th Rd.	44	B 3	Main Rd.	44	D 2	Scarboro Rd.	44	B 3	Station	44	D 2
d.	44	A 1	Marchmont Rd., off			School Rd.	44	C 2	Muizenberg Post Office	44	C 2
d.	44	A 1	Park Rd.	44	C 2	Scopus Rd.	44	C 2	Muizenberg		
d.	44	B 3	Maynard Rd.	44	C 3	Sea View Rd.	44	D 2	Primary School	44	C 2
Island Way	44	A 3	Melkboomweg	44	A 2	Sidmount Rd.	44	C 3	Star of the Sea		
on Rd.	44	C 3	Melrose Ave.	44	C 3	Somerset Cr.	44	A 2	Primary School	44	E 1
d.	44	A 2	Menton Rd.	44	E 1	Sorrento Rd.	44	E 1	Star of the Sea		
k Rd	44	C 3	Meulen Ct.	44	A 3	Spoon St.	44	A 1	Secondary School	44	E 3

TOURIST REGION - CAPE METROPOLITAN AREA
SIMON'S TOWN

Streets

NAME	PG	GRID	NAME	PG	GRID	NAME	PG	GRID	NAME	PG	GRID
			Dorion Cl.	45	E 3	Mariner's Cl.	45	C 1	Tredree Steps	45	E 3
			Duiker	45	A 1	Martello Rd.	45	E 3	Union St.	45	E 2
			Ferry Rd.	45	C 1	Nelson	45	E 2	Victory Cl.	45	E 1
Rd.	45	D 1	Flagship Way	45	E 2	Neptune Cl.	45	C 1	Victory La.	45	D 1
St.	45	E 1	Flora Steps	45	E 3	Nerine Steps	45	E 3	Victory Way	45	E 2
Rd.	45	E 3	Forest Hill Ave.	45	E 3	Osmond Cl.	45	C 1	Water La.	45	E 2
ters Cl.	45	B 1	Gannet	45	A 1	Palace Hill Rd.	45	D 1	Waterfall Rd.	45	D 1
.	45	E 1	Goede Gift Rd.	45	E 2	Paradise Rd.	45	C 1	Wilfred	45	E 1
eps	45	A 2	Harbour Heights Cl.	45	E 3	Penguin	45	A 1			
Rd.	45	D 1	Highlands La.	45	E 2	Pine	45	E 3	**General Information**		
a.	45	D 1	Hope St.	45	D 1	Quarry Rd.	45	D 2			
St.	45	E 2	Hopkirk Way	45	A 2	Reid's Way	45	A 1			
eps	45	E 3	Horatio	45	E 2	Ricketts Cl.	45	E 2	False Bay		
.	45	D 1	Jackson	45	E 2	Runciman Dr.	45	E 2	Yacht Club	45	D 2
nt Rd.	45	E 2	Jackson's Steps	45	E 2	Seemeeu	45	A 1	Simon's Town		
l St.	45	D 1	Jubilee St.	45	D 1	Smith's La.	45	E 2	Police Station	45	D 2
Rd.	45	C 1	Jurgens Rd.	45	A 1	St. George's St.	45	E 3	Simon's Town		
d.	45	D 1	Kemps Way	45	A 1	Station Rd.	45	D 1	Post Office	45	D 2
St.	45	D 1	King George's Way	45	E 2	Thomas St.	45	E 2	Simon's Town		
	45	E 2	Main Rd.	45	B 1	Trafalgar Pl.	45	E 2	Secondary School	45	E 3

TOURIST REGION - CAPE METROPOLITAN AREA
STRAND

Streets

NAME	PG	GRID	NAME	PG	GRID	NAME	PG	GRID	NAME	PG	GRID
			Altena Rd.	46	C 3	Beukes	46	C 1	Broeksman Cr.	46	A 2
			Amsterdam Cl.	46	A 3	Birkenhead St.	46	C 1	Burken St.	46	A 2
			Anderson	46	C 1	Boldcon	46	D 3	Burnard St.	46	C 1
Rd.	46	E 3	Arnoldt St.	46	B 3	Bosch St.	46	E 3	Calais Cl.	46	C 3
n St.	46	C 1	Athlone St.	46	A 3	Boschendal Rd.	46	B 3	Calvyn St.	46	B 3
ns Ave.	46	E 2	Auret	46	A 3	Boskloof St.	46	C 3	Church St.	46	B 2
e	46	E 2	Back La.	46	C 1	Bosman St.	46	A 2	Claassens Cl.	46	A 2
me Rd.	46	A 2	Baker St.	46	A 2	Boundary Rd.	46	D 3	Clarendon St.	46	A 3
t.	46	A 2	Beach Rd.	46	C 1	Brand St.	46	B 1	Compagne Cr.	46	A 2
St.	46	C 3	Belcher Cl.	46	A 2	Brewery Rd.	46	D 3	Conradie	46	D 2
	46	D 3	Benade St.	46	A 2	Broadway	46	A 2	Constantia St.	46	C 3

TOURIST REGION - CAPE METROPOLITAN AREA
STRAND
CONT.

TOURIST REGION - CAPE METROPOLITAN AREA
SOMERSET WEST

General Information

TOURIST REGION - CAPE METROPOLITAN AREA
ACCOMMODATION

Hotels

Other Accommodation

TOURIST REGION - CAPE METROPOLITAN AREA
PLACES OF INTEREST

TOURIST REGION - CAPE METROPOLITAN AREA
PLACES OF INTEREST cont.

NAME	PG	GRID	NAME	PG	GRID	NAME	PG	GRID	NAME	PG	GRID
beeck's Quarry slate used in at Cape Town)	36	E 3	Waterfall Walk	34	E 2	West Bathing Beach	34	C 3	World of Birds	34	D 2
egd Winery	34	A 3	Waterfront Craft Market	37	C 3	Wine Centre	37	B 1	World of Birds Wildlife Sanctuary	42	A 3
Church	36	D 3	Waterhof National Monument	38	E 2	Winton 1934 Shipwreck	34	D 1	Wynberg Park	34	D 2
Toy Museum n's Town)	45	D 2	Welmoed Winery	34	A 2	Wolfgat Nature Reserve	34	B 3	Zandvlei Bird Sanctuary	34	C 3
									Zevenwacht Winery	34	A 2

TOURIST REGION - WINELANDS
FRANSCHHOEK

Streets

NAME	PG	GRID	NAME	PG	GRID	NAME	PG	GRID	NAME	PG	GRID
St.	54	D 3	Disa St.	54	D 3	Lambrechts St.	54	E 3	Van Riebeeck St.	54	D 3
nie St.	54	C 2	East Reservoir	54	D 3	Louis Botha St.	54	D 2	Wilhelmina St.	54	D 2
Marie	54	D 1	Erica St.	54	D 3	Malherbe St.	54	C 2			
t.	54	E 2	Fabriek St.	54	D 2	Naude St.	54	C 2			
ux St.	54	D 2	Freesia St.	54	D 3	Nerina St.	54	D 3	**General Information**		
St.	54	D 2	Hauman St.	54	C 2	Pepler St.	54	C 1			
Hugo St.	54	D 2	Heide St.	54	D 3	Piere			Franschhoek Police Station	54	D 2
key St.	54	D 2	Huguenot	54	C 2	Jordaan St.	54	D 2	Franschhoek Post Office	54	D 2
ers	54	C 2	Huguenot	54	D 2	Protea St.	54	D 3	Franschhoek Secondary School	54	D 2
St.	54	C 2	Klein Cabriere St.	54	D 2	Reservoir St.	54	C 2	West End Primary School	54	C 2
ys St.	54	C 2	Klip St.	54	D 1	Roux St.	54	C 2			
			Kruger St.	54	D 2	Tuin St.	54	D 3			
			La Cotta St.	54	D 2	Uitkyk St.	54	C 2			
			La Rochelle St.	54	D 2	Union St.	54	D 3			

TOURIST REGION - WINELANDS
GORDON'S BAY

Streets

NAME	PG	GRID	NAME	PG	GRID	NAME	PG	GRID	NAME	PG	GRID
ls Way	55	B 3	Dennehof Dr.	55	C 3	Lancaster Rd.	55	B 1	St. Thomas Cl.	55	B 3
ss Way	55	B 3	Devon Rd.	55	C 2	Lemoenboom Rd.	55	B 3	Stinkhout Cl.	55	B 1
t.	55	A 1	Disa Rd.	55	B 1	Marais St.	55	D 2	Suikerbossie Dr.	55	E 1
Cl.	55	A 1	Dolphin Way	55	B 3	Marcus Cr.	55	B 2	Sunset Dr.	55	B 3
l.	55	B 2	Drake Cl.	55	C 2	Mariners Way	55	C 3	Swart St.	55	D 2
	55	B 2	Drommedaris St.	55	D 3	Melkboom Rd.	55	B 1	Swing Rd.	55	C 2
ai Cr.	55	B 1	Duiker Cl.	55	B 3	Mid Ocean Mews	55	B 2	Syringa Rd.	55	C 1
Dr.	55	D 3	East Cr.	55	C 2	Miller St.	55	D 2	Taaibos Rd.	55	C 2
rus St.	55	C 3	Eleventh	55	A 1	Milnerton Rd.	55	C 2	Trafalgar Rd.	55	B 3
e.	55	C 2	Essenhout St.	55	B 2	Mountain Rd.	55	D 2	Ulex Rd.	55	C 2
Rd.	55	D 2	Estoril Way	55	A 2	Mountain Valley Mews	55	A 2	Upper Watt St.	55	E 2
comber Cr.	55	C 3	Fairways Cl.	55	B 2	Nadia	55	A 1	Valley Cul de Sac	55	E 2
s Cl.	55	B 2	Farael	55	A 1	Nazli Way	55	A 1	Van der Byl St.	55	D 2
d.	55	B 2	Fatima	55	A 1	Nelson Cr.	55	B 3	Verbena Rd.	55	C 2
s Cl.	55	C 3	Faure Marine Dr.	55	B 1	Nemesia Rd.	55	C 2	Virgilia St.	55	B 1
Rd.	55	C 2	Faure St.	55	E 1	Neptunes Way	55	B 3	Vlier Cl.	55	B 1
St.	55	A 1	Firwood Way	55	B 2	Oak Rd.	55	C 1	Vygie Rd.	55	C 2
aters Way	55	B 3	Flamingo Cl.	55	B 3	Olienhout St.	55	B 1	Water Way	55	C 2
m Ave.	55	D 3	Galleon Cr.	55	B 3	Prunus Rd.	55	C 1	Watt St.	55	D 2
Locke Cl.	55	B 2	Garden Rd.	55	C 2	Quince Rd.	55	C 1	West Cr.	55	C 2
i Cl.	55	D 3	Gary Player Cl.	55	B 2	Restia Cl.	55	D 3	Whittle Cr.	55	B 2
vater La.	55	C 1	Geelhout Cl.	55	B 2	Riverside Ave.	55	C 2	Wildeboom Rd.	55	C 2
St.	55	C 3	Geldenhuys	55	A 1	Robina Rd.	55	C 1	Windjammer Rd.	55	C 3
tte St.	55	A 2	Glen Eagles Mews	55	A 2	Rooiels Cr.	55	B 1	Winged Foot Cl.	55	A 2
La.	55	D 2	Goeie Hoop St.	55	D 3	Roos St.	55	C 3	York Rd.	55	B 2
neer Way	55	C 3	Gondola Way	55	B 3	Ryger St.	55	D 3	Zeanette St.	55	A 1
Rd.	55	B 2	Gordonia Rd.	55	E 1	Sandpiper	55	B 3			
o Way	55	B 3	Green Way	55	C 3	School St.	55	B 3	**General Information**		
s Way	55	A 1	Grens Rd.	55	D 3	Sea Way	55	B 3			
res Cl.	55	B 2	Hahn Rd.	55	E 2	Seascape Cr.	55	B 3	Bay Crescent Kwik Spar Shopping Centre	55	C 2
an Ave.	55	D 3	Hibiscus Ave.	55	B 1	Seaview Cul de Sac	55	E 2	Gordon's Bay Boat Angling Club	55	C 1
La.	55	D 2	Iris Rd.	55	B 1	Sercor	55	A 1	Gordon's Bay Police Station	55	D 2
Cr.	55	C 2	Jakaranda Rd.	55	B 1	Shanghai Way	55	C 3	Gordon's Bay Post Office	55	D 2
d.	55	B 3	James Cl.	55	B 2	Shireen	55	A 1	Gordonsbaai Primary School	55	C 3
nion Way	55	B 3	Jannie Storm Rd.	55	D 2	Sir Lowry Rd.	55	D 2	Gustrow Sports Field	55	A 1
ss Cl.	55	B 2	Jannies Cl.	55	B 2	Smith St.	55	A 1	S.A. Naval College	55	E 1
all Rd.	55	B 2	Karee St.	55	B 1	Somerlust St.	55	C 2			
Cr.	55	A 1	Kerk St.	55	D 2	Somerset Rd.	55	C 2			
			Keurboom Rd.	55	B 1	Southern Cross Ave.	55	A 1			
			Kirby Rd.	55	C 2	St. Croix St.	55	B 3			
			Kloof Rd.	55	E 1	St. John Cl.	55	B 3			
			Laetitia	55	A 1						

TOURIST REGION - WINELANDS
PAARL

TOURIST REGION - WINELANDS
WELLINGTON

General Information

TOURIST REGION - WINELANDS
STELLENBOSCH

Streets

TOURIST REGION - WINELANDS
STELLENBOSCH CONT.

General Informati...

TOURIST REGION - WINELANDS
ACCOMMODATION

TOURIST REGION - WINELANDS
ACCOMMODATION cont.

TOURIST REGION - WINELANDS
PLACES OF INTEREST

TOURIST REGION - BREEDE RIVER VALLEY
MONTAGU cont.

PG	GRID	NAME	PG	GRID	NAME	PG	GRID	NAME
...t	69	C 2	Meul St	69	C 1	Thompson St	69	D 2
.....	69	B 1	Middel St	69	C 1	Unie St	69	C 2
...c	69	B 1	Park St	69	B 3	Van der		
...St	69	C 2	Piet Retief St	69	C 2	Merwe St	69	D 1
.....	69	C 2	Rossouw St	69	D 2	Van		
.....	69	B 1	Swanepoel St	69	D 2	Riebeeck St	69	D 2
...St	69	B 2	Tanner St	69	B 1	Van Zyl	69	D 2

General Information

NAME	PG	GRID
Montagu High	69	D 2
Montagu Police Station	69	C 3
Montagu Primary	69	C 2

TOURIST REGION - BREEDE RIVER VALLEY
ROBERTSON

Streets

PG	GRID	NAME	PG	GRID	NAME	PG	GRID	NAME	PG	GRID
.....	70	B 2	Drommedaris Ave	70	D 3	Malherbe St	70	C 1	Smith St	70	C 2
...e	70	B 2	Eben Donges Ave	70	D 2	Malva St	70	A 3	Solomon St	70	B 2
...y St	70	C 1	Elm Ave	70	D 3	Mark St	70	C 1	Sonneblom St	70	B 3
...St	70	B 3	Eluxolweni	70	E 3	Masakhane St	70	E 2	Sweetpea Ave	70	B 1
...ve	70	B 3	Erica St	70	A 2	Mbeki	70	E 3	Swellendam	70	C 1
...St	70	D 3	Ficus Ave	70	D 3	Meyer Cr.	70	B 2	Taaibos	70	A 2
... Ave	70	B 1	Fleur St	70	A 3	Mimosa Ave	70	B 1	Tienvoet St	70	B 2
...y St	70	B 2	Freema St	70	C 1	Muhafu St	70	E 3	Tindal St	70	B 2
.....	70	C 2	Freesia Ave	70	B 1	Muller St	70	A 3	Truter St	70	C 1
...ve	70	B 1	Geelhout Ave	70	D 3	Nassau Cr.	70	C 3	Tshazimpunzi	70	E 2
.....	70	E 3	George St	70	A 2	Neethling	70	C 2	Tulp St	70	B 3
...t	70	C 1	Goedehoop Ave	70	D 3	Nerina St	70	A 3	Uitnood St	70	C 1
...a St	70	A 3	Granaatbos	70	A 1	Ntlakotlala	70	E 3	Van der Stel St	70	C 1
...St	70	A 2	Gum Grove St	70	C 3	October St	70	B 3	Van Graan St	70	C 3
.....	70	E 3	Hager Ave	70	B 2	Orley St	70	B 3	Van Oudtshoorn St	70	C 3
...n Ave	70	D 3	Hani St	70	E 2	Paddy St	70	A 2	Van Rheenen St	70	C 1
...nbos	70	A 2	Heide Ave	70	B 2	Papawer St	70	B 1	Van Riebeeck Ave	70	D 3
...s	70	A 2	Heuwel St	70	A 3	Parel Ave	70	C 3	Van Zyl St	70	B 1
...bos	70	A 2	Hibiscus Ave	70	B 1	Park St	70	B 2	Victoria St	70	C 1
...wel Ave	70	C 3	Hokim St	70	B 2	Paul Kruger St	70	C 2	Viola Ave	70	B 1
...St	70	C 3	Hoop St	70	C 1	Peperbos	70	A 2	Voortrekker Rd	70	D 1
...na	70	E 3	Hopley Ave	70	B 1	Petunia St	70	B 3	Vygie St	70	B 2
...Ave	70	D 3	Hospital Ave	70	B 2	Piet Retief St	70	C 2	Warren St	70	C 2
...n Ave	70	B 1	Industria St	70	E 2	Pietersen St	70	B 3	Waterkant St	70	C 2
...ux St	70	C 1	Iris St	70	A 3	Polack St	70	C 2	Watsonia St	70	B 3
...e St	70	B 2	Jakaranda Ave	70	D 2	Protea Ave	70	A 2	Waveren St	70	C 3
...St	70	A 2	Jansen Cr.	70	B 3	Reitz St	70	C 2	Wesley St	70	B 2
...ntia St	70	C 1	Japonika St	70	B 3	Richter St	70	B 3	White St	70	C 1
...ek St	70	A 3	Jasmyn St	70	A 3	Rijger Ave	70	D 3	Willem Nel St	70	C 1
...St	70	B 3	Johnson St	70	B 2	Rivier St	70	B 2			
.....	70	E 3	Jones St	70	A 3	Robertson	70	C 1			
...ers St	70	B 2	Jubel St	70	A 2	Rolbos	70	A 1			
...t St	70	B 2	Kerk St	70	D 2	Rolbos	70	A 2			
...t St	70	B 3	Klapperbos	70	A 2	Roodezand St	70	C 3			
...Ave	70	D 3	Kloof St	70	B 3	Rooibroodbos	70	A 2			
...Jys St	70	D 2	Konstitutie St	70	C 1	Roos St	70	A 3			
...ve	70	B 1	Kort St	70	E 2	Rosa Ave	70	B 1			
...cht Ave	70	C 2	Lang St	70	E 2	Rosita St	70	B 3			
...bos	70	A 2	Langeberg St	70	A 3	Saayman St	70	B 3			
			Le Roux St	70	B 1	Sainsbury St	70	B 2			
			Leeubekkie Ave	70	B 1	Samuel St	70	E 3			
			Leeuwin Ave	70	C 3	Scafie St	70	A 2			
			Loop St	70	B 2	Silimela St	70	E 3			
			Lusernbos	70	A 2	Smal St	70	C 1			

General Information

NAME	PG	GRID
Dagbreek School	70	A 2
De Villiers Primary	70	B 2
Hoerskool Robertson	70	D 2
Information Bureau	70	C 1
Laerskool Robertson	70	D 2
Langeberg School	70	A 2
Robertson Hospital	70	C 2
Robertson Police Station	70	D 1
Robertson Post Office	70	C 1
Vergesig Primary	70	A 2

TOURIST REGION - BREEDE RIVER VALLEY
WORCESTER

Streets

PG	GRID	NAME	PG	GRID	NAME	PG	GRID	NAME	PG	GRID
...om St	71	B 1	Bergsig	71	C 1	De Wet St	71	B 3	Fairbairn St	71	B 2
...ey St	71	C 2	Bird La.	71	B 2	Deon Britz St	71	E 2	Fairbairn St Ext.	71	B 3
...Ave	71	B 3	Bonus St	71	C 3	Dirk Brand St	71	E 3	Fairy Glen	71	C 1
...yn St	71	B 3	Bosman St	71	D 2	Disa St	71	C 1	Field St	71	A 1
...raven Cr.	71	E 2	Botha Cr.	71	E 2	Distillery Rd	71	E 3	Fisher St	71	A 3
...St	71	C 3	Butler St	71	E 2	Dommisse St	71	D 2	Fransman St	71	A 2
...St	71	C 1	Central	71	C 2	Du Toit Ave	71	D 2	Freislich St	71	D 2
...t	71	C 2	Cilliers St	71	D 2	Durban St	71	B 3	Frere St	71	D 2
...St	71	C 2	Cole St	71	E 2	E. Philcox St	71	D 1	Gie	71	D 2
...y St	71	E 2	Combrink St	71	A 2	Eich St	71	D 1	Governer St	71	E 2
...St	71	D 2	Cradock St	71	E 2	Elmboos La.	71	D 3	Grey St	71	B 3
...os St	71	C 1	De Lat Bat Rd	71	B 1	Engelbrecht St	71	C 1	Hartwig Ave	71	A 3
			De Villiers St	71	D 2	Erica St	71	B 1	Heath St	71	C 1
			De VosSt	71	D 3	Esselenpark	71	A 3	Hendry Coert	71	B 3
			De Waal St	71	C 1	F. Auden St	71	D 1	Hendry Gird St	71	D 2

TOURIST REGION - BREEDE RIVER VALLEY
WORCESTER CONT.

TOURIST REGION - BREEDE RIVER VALLEY
ACCOMMODATION

TOURIST REGION - BREEDE RIVER VALLEY
PLACES OF INTEREST

TOURIST REGION - BREEDE RIVER VALLEY
PLACES OF INTEREST cont.

TOURIST REGION - WEST COAST
MALMESBURY

TOURIST REGION - WEST COAST
MALMESBURY cont.

NAME	PG	GRID	NAME	PG	GRID	NAME	PG	GRID	NAME	PG	GRID
Verbena	78	E 2	Wagener St	78	B 3	**General Information**			St Thomas Primary School	7	
Verdmuller St	78	C 2	Wandel St	78	C 2				Swartland Hoërskool	7	
Victoria St	78	B 3	Watsonia Ave	78	E 2	Malmesbury Police Station	78	B 1	Swartland Hospital/Clinic	7	
Vinkel	78	D 3	West St	78	C 2	Malmesbury Post Office	78	B 2	Swartland Laerskool	7	
Viola Ave	78	D 2	Wilger St	78	E 2	Skoonspruit Hoërskool	78	D 2	Tafelzicht Fire Station	7	
Voortrekker Rd	78	B 3	Wistaria	78	C 2	Skoonspruit Laerskool	78	D 2	Wesbank Sekondere Skool	7	
Vos St	78	C 2	Ysterhout	78	E 2						
Vrede St	78	A 2	Zinnia Ave	78	E 3						
Waboom Ave	78	E 2	Zola St	78	E 3						

TOURIST REGION - WEST COAST
VREDENBURG

Streets

NAME	PG	GRID	NAME	PG	GRID	NAME	PG	GRID	NAME	PG	GRID
			Elsie	79	E 3	Kwartel	79	E 3	Sydney Rule	7	
			Erica	79	C 3	Lang	79	C 2	Sysie	7	
			Esperia	79	B 2	Langeberg	79	A 1	Taurus	7	
Abdol	79	D 2	Factory	79	B 2	Leyden	79	B 1	Theefontein	7	
Adelaar	79	D 3	Fairbairn	79	D 2	Link Skakel	79	C 3	Third	7	
Adelaar	79	E 3	Fifth	79	D 2	Lisboa	79	D 1	Tortelduif	7	
Akkerdyk	79	B 1	Fisante	79	D 3	Lochner	79	B 1	Turner	7	
Angelier	79	C 3	Floryn	79	E 1	Loerie	79	D 3	Uitspan	7	
Apollo	79	B 2	Fourth	79	D 2	Long	79	C 2	Unie	7	
Appies	79	E 3	Francois Pienaar	79	B 1	Loubser	79	C 1	Valk	7	
Arendse	79	C 2	Frederick	79	B 1	Maclons	79	D 3	Van Enkhuizen	7	
Athena	79	B 2	Gamaring	79	D 1	Main	79	C 1	Van Linschoten	7	
Atlas	79	B 2	Gans	79	E 3	Marigold	79	C 3	Van Molbergen	7	
Berg	79	D 1	Geelwou	79	E 3	Mark	79	C 2	Van Riebeeck	7	
Berghaan	79	E 3	Helderberg	79	D 2	Nassau	79	B 1	Van Schalkwyk	7	
Bergsig	79	D 2	Hendricks	79	D 3	Nerina	79	B 1	Van Spilbergen	7	
Bester	79	C 3	Herme	79	B 1	Noordhoek	79	C 2	Van Zyl	7	
Binnering	79	C 1	Heuningklip	79	C 2	Olympia	79	B 2	Velddrif	7	
Bloemhof	79	C 1	Hill	79	C 1	Ooievaar	79	D 3	Vink	7	
Bloureier	79	E 3	Hospital	79	C 2	Oranje	79	D 2	Volstruis	7	
Boog	79	C 1	Hout	79	C 1	Oxford	79	D 2	Vraagom	7	
Boom	79	D 2	Houtkapper	79	E 2	Park	79	C 1	Vrede	7	
Boswewer	79	D 3	Houtman	79	D 1	Pasteur	79	B 2	Waterkant	7	
Bougainvillae	79	D 3	Ibis	79	B 2	Piet My Vrou	79	D 3	Witteklip	7	
Bowers	79	E 3	Industry	79	C 3	Piet Retief	79	B 1	Yale	7	
Bree	79	C 1	Iona	79	B 2	Plein	79	C 1	Zeeburg	7	
Buren	79	B 1	Ixia	79	B 1	Pou	79	E 2			
Cambridge	79	D 2	Jacob Sadie	79	C 2	Primrose	79	D 3	**General Informati**		
Cedras	79	D 2	James Small	79	B 2	Proses	79	C 2			
Church	79	B 1	Jasmyn	79	C 3	Rand	79	D 1	Karitas Secondary School	79	
Cloete	79	D 2	Joel Stransky	79	B 1	Robel	79	E 1	Panorama Primary School	79	
Da Gama	79	D 1	Joubert	79	C 2	Rooihals	79	E 3	Vredenburg Hoër en Laerskool	79	
Dalmeida	79	D 1	Julius	79	D 2	Salamander	79	B 1	Vredenburg Hospital	79	
De Beer	79	D 2	Kanarie	79	D 3	Saldanha	79	D 2	Vredenburg Information Centre	79	
De Jongh	79	D 2	Keyzerskraal	79	B 1	School	79	C 1	Vredenburg Police Station	79	
De Klip	79	C 1	Kiewiet	79	A 2	Second	79	D 2	Vredenburg Post Office	79	
Diaz	79	D 1	Klein Witteklip	79	C 1	Seemeeu	79	D 3	West Coast Private Hospital	79	
Dirkie Uys	79	C 2	Klipfontein	79	A 1	Seventh	79	D 3	Weston Hoërskool	79	
Disa	79	B 1	Kloof	79	D 1	Sixth	79	D 2			
Dobbertjie	79	E 3	Klooftjieskloof	79	D 3	Smit	79	D 2			
Dorp	79	C 1	Kootjieskloof	79	C 2	Spreeu	79	D 2			
Draai	79	A 1	Kort	79	D 2	Spreeu	79	E 2			
Dreyer	79	D 2	Korthaan	79	B 1	Steenberg	79	B 1			
Duif	79	D 3	Koster	79	C 2	Stephan	79	C 2			
Eend	79	E 3	Kraai	79	E 2	Sterling	79	E 1			
Ellenboog	79	D 1	Kraanvoël	79	E 2	Swart	79	D 2			

TOURIST REGION - WEST COAST
CLANWILLIAM

Streets

NAME	PG	GRID	NAME	PG	GRID	NAME	PG	GRID	NAME	P
			Buitenkant St	84	C 2	Hennie du Plessis Cl.	84	E 2	Main Rd	84
			Denne St	84	C 2	Hibuskus St	84	D 2	Market St	84
			Deon Burger Rd	84	C 2	Hospital St	84	B 1	Meissenheimer	84
			Devlei St	84	A 1	Jakaranda St	84	C 2	Milner St	84
Aandblom St	84	C 2	Disa Ave	84	C 2	Katjiepiering St	84	C 1	Nerina St	84
Alheit St	84	B 1	Dwars St	84	D 2	Kersbos Ave	84	D 2	Nortier St	84
Anemoon Ave	84	D 2	Eike Ave	84	C 2	Leipoldt St	84	B 2	Old Cape Rd	84
Arnold St	84	B 2	Flip Lochner Cr.	84	E 2	Long St	84	B 1	Orange St	84
Augsburg St	84	B 2	Foster Rd	84	B 2	Love Cr.	84	C 2	Park Rd	84
Azalia Ave	84	D 2	Freesia Ave	84	A 1	Love St	84	C 2	President Brand St	84
Bergsig St	84	A 2	Gousblom Ave	84	D 2	Magnolia Ave	84	D 2	Protea St	84
Bloekom Ave	84	C 2	Graafwater Rd	84	A 1					

TOURIST REGION - WEST COAST
CLANWILLIAM cont.

NAME	PG GRID	NAME	PG GRID	NAME	PG GRID
el St	84 C 2	Sitrus St	84 B 2	Voortrekker Rd	84 B 2
m St	84 B 1	Sonneblom St	84 D 2	Waboom St	84 C 2
oke St	84 B 1	Strassberger	84 E 2	Waterblom St	84 C 2
on St	84 B 2	Suikerbos Ave	84 D 2	Watsonia St	84 C 2
Ave	84 C 1	Syringa Ave	84 D 2	Wilge Ave	84 D 2
au St	84 B 1	Van Reenen St	84 A 1	Willem	
t	84 C 1	Viooltjie St	84 C 2	Carstens Ave	84 E 2
ve	84 C 2	Visser Rd	84 B 2	Willie van Zyl Cl.	84 E 2

General Information

NAME	PG GRID
Clanwilliam Hospital	84 C 2
Clanwilliam Information Office	84 B 2
Clanwilliam Police Station	84 B 2

TOURIST REGION - WEST COAST
LAMBERT'S BAY

Streets

NAME	PG GRID	NAME	PG GRID	NAME	PG GRID	NAME	PG GRID
St	85 C 2	Fisant St	85 C 2	Malkopbaai St	85 C 1	Stelano St	85 D 1
St	85 C 1	Fisher St	85 C 1	Maritz St	85 B 3	Stephan St	85 B 3
St	85 C 2	Fransman St	85 C 2	Morn St	85 C 1	Strand St	85 D 1
nhout St	85 C 2	Hoof St	85 C 1	Otterdam St	85 B 3	Sybil St	85 C 1
St	85 C 2	Hoog St	85 D 1	Paul Kruger St	85 B 2	Taylor	85 C 2
St	85 C 1	Johnson St	85 D 2	Pelikaan St	85 C 2	Tollies St	85 B 2
St	85 D 2	Joubert	85 C 2	Pretorius St	85 B 2	Van Zyl St	85 C 1
St	85 D 2	Kerk St	85 C 1	Quickfall St	85 C 2	Voortrekker St	85 B 2
e St	85 C 2	Koporasie St	85 B 2	Riedeman St	85 B 1	Voortrekker St	85 C 1
lan St	85 C 1	Kortier St	85 B 2	Ruiter St	85 C 2	Yisser St	85 C 1
St	85 B 2	Lang St	85 C 1	School St	85 B 2		
St	85 C 1	Leipoldt St	85 C 1	Seemeeu St	85 D 2		
St	85 C 1	Lizzie Brett St	85 C 2	Spence St	85 B 3		
		Main St	85 C 1	St Mark St	85 D 2		
		Malgas St	85 C 2	St Peter St	85 D 2		
		Malgas St	85 D 1	Stanley St	85 C 2		

General Information

NAME	PG GRID
Lambert's Bay Police Station	85 B 1

TOURIST REGION - WEST COAST
VREDENDAL

Streets

NAME	PG GRID	NAME	PG GRID	NAME	PG GRID	NAME	PG GRID
St	86 B 1	Eike St	86 B 2	Noord Rd	86 A 2	Tuin St	86 B 3
St	86 A 3	Goedehoop St	86 D 1	Oleander St	86 B 1	Van der Stel St	86 B 2
nof	86 B 2	Grens St	86 B 2	Park St	86 B 2	Van Riebeek	86 B 2
	86 B 1	Hibiscus St	86 B 1	Pastorie St	86 B 2	Voortrekker	86 B 2
Cl.	86 C 2	Hoek St	86 A 3	Penkop St	86 B 3	Vrede St	86 D 1
Cr.	86 C 1	Hospitaal St	86 C 2	Pinotage St	86 C 2	Waterkant St	86 B 3
k St	86 B 3	Hospital St	86 C 2	Plataan St	86 B 1	Wes	86 C 1
St	86 B 1	Impala St	86 C 3	Plein St	86 C 2		
St	86 D 2	Karee St	86 C 1	Protea St	86 B 3		
e St	86 C 1	Kerk St	86 B 2	Rand St	86 B 2		
bar St	86 C 2	Kooperasie St	86 B 3	Riesling St	86 D 2		
g St	86 C 3	Koper St	86 C 1	Rivier St	86 A 3		
St	86 B 2	Kort St	86 B 3	Rugby St	86 C 2		
t	86 C 2	Kristal St	86 B 3	Saffier Cr.	86 B 3		
nt St	86 C 1	Laborie Cr.	86 C 2	Sentraal St	86 B 3		
t	86 B 3	Lausan Rd	86 B 1	Shiraz Cl.	86 C 2		
		Loop St	86 B 3	Skool St	86 B 2		
		Middel St	86 C 2	Stein St	86 D 2		
		Mohasiet	86 C 2	Sultan St	86 B 3		

General Information

NAME	PG GRID
Information Bureau	86 A 3
Vredendal High	86 B 2
Vredendal Hospital/Clinic	86 C 2
Vredendal Police Station	86 A 3
Vredendal Primary School	86 B 2

TOURIST REGION - WEST COAST
VANRHYNSDORP

Streets

NAME	PG GRID	NAME	PG GRID	NAME	PG GRID
ercial	87 C 3	Mission	87 C 2	Skool	87 B 2
	87 B 1	Namakwa	87 C 2	Troe Troe	87 B 2
	87 C 3	Olive	87 C 2	Vaal	87 B 2
ama	87 C 2	Paddock	87 B 2	Van Riebeeck	87 C 1
		Residential	87 C 3	Van Zyl	87 B 1
		Rivierkant	87 C 2	Voortrekker	87 C 1

General Information

NAME	PG GRID
Vanrhynsdorp Information Centre	87 C 2
Vanrhynsdorp Police Station	87 C 2

TOURIST REGION - WEST COAST
ACCOMMODATION

TOURIST REGION - WEST COAST
PLACES OF INTEREST

TOURIST REGION - OVERBERG
BREDASDORP

Streets

NAME	PG	GRID	NAME	PG	GRID	NAME	PG	GRID
			Du Toit St	94	C 1	Matthees St	94	D 1	Swarthout Cr.	94	D 1

General Information

TOURIST REGION - OVERBERG
CALEDON

Streets

General Information

TOURIST REGION - OVERBERG
HERMANUS

Streets

TOURIST REGION - OVERBERG
HERMANUS

NAME	PG	GRID	NAME	PG	GRID	NAME	PG	GRID	NAME
Nichol	96	C 1	Rocklands	96	E 2	Stemmet	96	C 2	Hermanus
Northway	96	D 1	Royal	96	D 2	Talana	96	E 1	Hospital
Orothamus	96	E 2	Scout	96	C 1	Theron	96	A 2	Hermanus
Oveday	96	E 2	Sea	96	C 2	Waboom	96	B 1	Information Centre ...
Paterson	96	D 2	Seeberg	96	E 2	Walker Bay	96	A 1	Hermanus
Plein	96	E 2	Selkirk	96	B 1	Westcliff	96	E 2	Police Station
Protea	96	C 2	Smuts	96	E 2				Hermanus Post
Raed na Gael	96	A 1	Spence	96	D 2	**General Information**			Office
Regent	96	D 1	St Peters	96	D 2				Hermanus
Robin	96	E 1	Steenbok	96	D 1	Hermanus High School	96	C 1	Primary School

TOURIST REGION - OVERBERG
SWELLENDAM

NAME	PG	GRID	NAME	PG	GRID	NAME	PG	GRID	NAME
Streets			Freesia St	97	E 2	Nelson St	97	B 2	Trui St
			Fullard St	97	C 2	Nerina St	97	D 2	Uitsig Ave
			Glen Barry Rd	97	A 3	Oak St	97	D 2	Van Blommenstein St ..
Aanhuizen St	97	B 1	Groenenald St	97	B 3	Ondendaal St	97	C 1	Van der Walt St
Akasia Ave	97	D 2	Guaelberg St	97	A 3	Palm St	97	D 2	Van Dyk St
Alice St	97	B 1	Heemrand St	97	B 3	Panorama Rd	97	B 1	Van Eenden St
Alwyn St	97	D 2	Heide Ave	97	D 2	Peckham St	97	A 2	Van Immhof St
Andrew Whyte St	97	B 1	Hermanus Steyn St	97	B 3	Pekeur St	97	D 2	Van Oudtshoorn Rd ...
Anemoon St	97	E 2	Heyns St	97	B 3	Petunia St	97	E 2	Van Ryneveld St
Athlone St	97	B 1	High St	97	E 2	Plein St	97	A 2	Van Staden St
Auge St	97	A 3	Holster St	97	D 2	Pont St	97	E 1	Van Zyl St
Baker St	97	B 2	Hopley St	97	D 2	President St	97	D 1	Veldkornet St
Bazania St	97	E 2	Hout St	97	B 1	Protea Ave	97	D 2	Visser St
Belderblom St	97	B 2	Iris Cr.	97	E 2	Queens St	97	E 2	Von Manber St
Berea St	97	B 2	Jakaranda St	97	C 2	Reid St	97	B 3	Voortrek St
Berg St	97	A 3	Kamp St	97	B 3	Reitz St	97	B 2	Vysie St
Bontebok St	97	D 2	Kanon St	97	A 2	Republiek St	97	D 1	William Robertson St ..
Brown St	97	C 2	Karb St	97	D 1	Resiebaan St	97	D 2	
Buirski St	97	B 1	Keerom St	97	B 3	Resiebaan St	97	D 2	**General Informat...**
Buitekant St	97	B 2	Kerk St	97	B 3	Rhenius St	97	B 2	
Coldrey St	97	B 1	Kerkplein	97	A 2	Ring St	97	D 2	
Commisioner St	97	C 1	Klipheuwel St	97	D 2	Roos St	97	D 2	Bontebok Primary
Cooper St	97	D 1	Kloof St	97	B 2	Rothman St	97	E 1	School
Coronation St	97	D 2	Kollebe St	97	C 1	Scholtz St	97	B 2	Olyfkrans College
Cyprug St	97	A 2	Kort St	97	B 2	Shand St	97	A 2	Swellendam
Daffodil St	97	E 2	Koster St	97	A 2	Siebelaar St	97	D 2	High School
Dahlia St	97	E 2	Lelie St	97	E 2	Siebert St	97	B 2	Swellendam Hospital ...
De Wist St	97	B 2	Lind St	97	C 1	Skool St	97	B 1	Swellendam
Delaport St	97	A 3	Lourens St	97	C 2	Sofietjie St	97	D 2	Information Centre ...
Delphinium St	97	E 2	May St	97	C 2	Somerset St	97	C 2	Swellendam
Die Rand St	97	B 1	Maynier St	97	D 1	Sonneblom St	97	E 2	Police Station
Disa St	97	D 2	Meltevreden St	97	A 2	Stasie St	97	C 2	Swellendam
Drostoy St	97	B 3	Meul St	97	D 1	Steil St	97	B 2	Post Office
Du Toit St	97	B 1	Meyer St	97	D 2	Streicher St	97	C 1	Swellendam
Edelweis St	97	D 2	Moolman St	97	C 1	Swellengrebel St	97	B 3	Primary School
Ellis St	97	C 3	Mozambique St	97	A 1	Theunissen St	97	C 2	Swellendam
Erika St	97	E 2	Muller St	97	B 1	Tilney St	97	A 3	Secondary School ...
Fairsairn St	97	B 2	Murray St	97	B 1	Tomlinson St	97	B 3	Swellenduimpie
Faure St	97	A 3	Myburgh St	97	C 1	Trichardt St	97	B 2	Primary School

TOURIST REGION - OVERBERG
ACCOMMODATION

NAME	PG	GRID	NAME	PG	GRID	NAME	PG	GRID	NAME
Hotels			Napier	92	C 2	Anlou	91	C 4	Die Voorhuis
			Old Stanford Inn	91	B 5	Annie's Annie	94	D 1	Ear of Clarendon
			Overberg Hotel	95	B 3	Arniston Seaside			Earl of Clarendon
Alexandra	91	A 5	Parkland	91	A 5	Cottages	93	D 4	Elim Caravan Park
Alexandra Hotel	95	C 2	Standard	92	C 3	Bellavista	91	C 5	Elim Lodge
Arniston	93	D 4	Standard	94	C 1	Birkenhead Lodge	91	D 4	Fair Hill
Beach House on			Stanford House	91	C 5	Blue Crane	92	C 2	Fairfields
Sandown Bay	90	B 2	Struisbaai	92	E 3	Buçaco Sud	90	B 2	Habour Lights
Bot River	90	A 3	Victoria	92	C 3	Chesham	96	A 2	Hame with House
Caledon Casino Hotel			Victoria	94	C 1	Coach House	94	D 1	Haus Barbara
and Spa	91	A 5	Windsor	91	B 4	De Twee Heeren	94	C 1	Haus Bavaria
De Kelders	91	C 5	Windsor Hotel	96	D 2	De Volkshuis	94	C 1	Haus Windhoek
Gansbaai Sea View	91	C 4				Die Dam			Hermanus
Herberg	93	D 4	**Other Accommodation**			Holiday Resort			Hermanus Esplanade ..
Marine	91	B 4				& Caravan Park	92	E 1	Heuningberghuisie
Marine Hotel	96	C 2	19th Hole	96	B 2	Die Kelders	91	C 5	Hortensia Lodge

TOURIST REGION - OVERBERG
ACCOMMODATION cont.

TOURIST REGION - OVERBERG
PLACES OF INTEREST

TOURIST REGION - CENTRAL KAROO
BEAUFORT WEST

TOURIST REGION - CENTRAL KAROO
LAINGSBURG

TOURIST REGION - CENTRAL KAROO
ACCOMMODATION

TOURIST REGION - CENTRAL KAROO
PLACES OF INTEREST

TOURIST REGION - KLEIN KAROO
OUDTSHOORN

Streets

TOURIST REGION - KLEIN KAROO
ACCOMMODATION

Hotels

TOURIST REGION - KLEIN KAROO
ACCOMMODATION CONT.

TOURIST REGION - KLEIN KAROO
PLACES OF INTEREST

TOURIST REGION - GARDEN ROUTE
GEORGE

TOURIST REGION - GARDEN ROUTE
GEORGE cont.

TOURIST REGION - GARDEN ROUTE
KNYSNA

TOURIST REGION - GARDEN ROUTE
MOSSEL BAY

TOURIST REGION - GARDEN ROUTE
PLETTENBERG BAY

TOURIST REGION - GARDEN ROUTE
ACCOMMODATION

TOURIST REGION - GARDEN ROUTE
ACCOMMODATION cont.

TOURIST REGION - GARDEN ROUTE
PLACES OF INTEREST

ACKNOWLEDGEMENTS
Photographic Credits
Walter Knirr

Cover: Chapman's Peak Drive
Page II - Disa, "La Dauphine" and Gannets
Page III - Karoo Botanical Gardens, "Heerengracht"
Page IV - Holy Trinity Church, Sunset, Kirstenbosch Botanical Gardens
Page 2 - Wheat fields
Page 3 - Cape Agulhas Lighthouse
Page 10 - Beacon Isle Hotel
Page 20 - Maltese Cross
Page 32 - Table Mountain
Page 35 - Penguins
Page 48 - Drying fruit
Page 60 - The Breede River
Page 72 - Ramskop Nature Reserve
Page 76 - Langebaan lagoon
Page 88 - Waenhuiskrans
Page 98 - The Karoo
Page 104 - Ostrich riding
Page 110 - Outeniqua "Choo Tjoe"
Page 113 - Tsitsikamma National Park

Copy supplied by the Western Cape Tourism Board. www.capetourism.org

Cartography
Annette Thomas
Barbara Brightwell
Deon Kok
Thomas Rodger
Nishaan Mathadeen

Research
Christopher Hosken

Design
Tina Pretorius

Advertising
Sonja Strydom

Index
Tina Pretorius
Benita Kandia

AMENDMENTS ?

As part of our ongoing product improvement programme, we value your input. This information together with your personal details (name, address and occupation) can be sent **Post Free** to the following address.

Freepost JHZ 4417
Attention: The Research Department
Map Studio
P.O. Box 277
RIVONIA, 2128

Tel. (011) 807-2292
Fax. (011) 807-0409
E-mail Address: research@mapstudio.co.za